SO YOU WANNA BE A SOAPMAKER!

The Definitive Beginners Guide
Turning Your Dream Into a 6-figure Successful
Business From Startup to Making and Selling
Your First Bar of All-Natural Soap and Beyond

Brian Cockell

Brian Cockell
website at www.lifegevitysoaps.ca

First Printing: October 2021

ISBN - 978-1-7771118-0-9

Contents

ABOUT THE AUTHOR

Brian Cockell - Executive, Chief Operating Officer of one of Canada's largest private companies left behind to become an artisan soap and skincare maker. Loves are teaching, researching, engineering, science, and making spectacular handcrafted natural soap, skin, hair, and lip care products and running LifeGevity Soap Company Inc.

Married to Fonda with seven children, ten grandchildren, eight Maremma sheepdogs, and one cat. We live on 160 acres in the middle of nowhere off-the-grid deep in Northern Ontario, Canada, trying our hand at homesteading.

To try the soap listed in the recipe in this book, follow our homesteading adventure, or to just pop in to say hi, visit:

To try the soap listed in the recipe in this book, follow our homesteading adventure, or to just pop in to say hi, visit:

www.lifegevitysoaps.ca

WHO THIS BOOK IS WRITTEN FOR

So, if you are reading this, you are probably interested in becoming a soapmaker or at least exploring the possibilities. This book is for those aspiring to start a soapmaking business, Homesteaders or Off-Gridders looking to become self-sufficient, new, or existing soapmakers looking to increase their skill level or those who want to learn how to make great soap for home, family, and fun.

—BRIAN COCKELL

WHY ANOTHER SOAP BOOK

Over the years, I have come to realize that as they say, "You are what you eat" also applies to "You are what you put on your body, head, and lips." As a researcher, it became clear that we are not doing any favours for ourselves by dosing our bodies in cocktails of synthetic chemicals, artificial dyes, toxins, and known carcinogens found in most conventional skin, hair, and lip care products. I set out to understand what all this meant for us. It became clear that corporate profits and slick advertising campaigns were winning the day. The conclusion was terrible news for our well-being and long-term health, not to mention the environment.

I set out to go all-natural and found many great natural soap, skin, hair, and lip products with varying degrees of "Natural" but did not find what I considered the perfect natural product. I found many products comprised of filler oils with the good stuff listed as footnotes at the end of the ingredients list or scented with synthetic fragrance and so forth. Most continue to waste our resources with unnecessary outer packaging, plastic wraps, and blister packs. Many of the larger Natural Artisan Soap Companies that were doing a great job have sold out to large corporations. If you look at their ingredients list, from their original products to the new owners' changes, you will be amazed. Premium ingredients are now footnotes. These sellouts help open the door for new and innovative natural soapmakers to enter the market. It became clear to me that someone making a natural product is not necessarily making a great product. I decided that someone would be me.

Enter the science of soap. Ten years of research learning how to set up a business and comply with government regulations in product and packaging development. Learning about packaging, labelling, production methods, production tools, marketing methods, shipping methods. Learning the different techniques of producing handcrafted artisan soap. Learning the properties of fatty acids (triglycerides) in oils and different kinds of butter, the therapeutic benefits of each essential oil and studying botanical additives and learning what properties they impart to soaps. For ten years before I ever made my first bar of soap, I read and studied every book, blog, and internet article I could find on the above topics. The problem was, I bought every book I could find on the subjects, but I was never able to find a good book that comprehensively covered even close to what I was seeking to accomplish, starting an artisan soap company from scratch. I found good books on individual elements, but a comprehensive tutorial did not exist.

After ten years of study, I made my first bar of soap. 1000's of recipe experiments later, hounding friends, family, and coworkers for years to try this, try that, fill out my survey. I believed I had formulated the most spectacular natural soap available on the market today. The adventure of LifeGevity Soap Company Inc. thus began in 2016. Know, my wife and I enjoy every aspect of life, doing what we love, and loving what we do!

The purpose of this book is to share my experiences and knowledge through this journey and hopefully save you some of the pain, frustrations, and time-wasting activities I went through to get here. I will cover every aspect of starting a soap company, including covering all of the topics above and sharing the recipes I have developed over the years as a starting point for you to kick off your soapmaking adventure. You will find all the information you will need right here. This book is a comprehensive learning guide from start to finish.

Let your journey begin!

—BRIAN COCKELL

Dedication

I dedicate this book to my loving, patient wife, Fonda, for putting up with the countless hours over the years I have spent with my nose in books or over beakers. For putting up with and trying to listen with interest as I rambled on about saponification, triglycerides, carcinogens, this recipe idea, that label idea, this or that product name, and the list goes on.

Baby, you are a trooper and my everything!
All my love! Brian.
XOXOXOXO

WHERE DO YOU START
Considerations

"The secret to getting ahead is getting started."
—Mark Twain

SO, YOU WANT TO BE A SOAPMAKER: great news, and how exciting. There is nothing more gratifying than creating your first bar of soap, taking in the beautiful scents you have created, and having that first bath or shower with your new creation. A sense of joy and accomplishment comes over you, and your skin feels oh so soft and smells wonderful. What an accomplishment, but where do you go from here. There are a couple of things you need to take into consideration and make decisions on as you begin to plan your journey. I will touch on each one and go into more depth on each consideration as we travel through the chapters.

Consideration 1 – What Type of Soapmaker Do You Want To Be

The first consideration is to determine what type of soapmaker you want to be. Yes, there is more than one type. I wish someone had sat me down and explained this before I began, but I never found this topic in a single book. I have defined the different soapmakers into three types and identified them as Hobbyist, Novelty, and Functional. Let's take a look at each type. You will need to fit into either one category or a combination of two. You cant be all three.

The Hobbyist soapmaker is someone who still has a day job but wants to make soap for themselves for various reasons. Some reasons might be to start to go all-natural and remove the synthetics, nasty chemicals, carcinogens, and toxins from their daily routine. Another reason might be the joy of learning a new skill. Maybe the goal is to dabble a little to see if soapmaking is the right fit for them to start a small business. Independent of the reason, the hobbyist is not setting out to start a business on day one or get too heavily involved in the activity of making soap. The hobbyist will scour the internet and soap books for recipes and how-to books. They will generally start by making it for friends, family, and themselves in small batches. They will ultimately begin to sell a bar or two at the church bazaar, local legion, or around their neighbourhood. Most hobbyists will make soap in their kitchen and only produce small batches. Some will buy a melt and pour base; we will discuss this in a bit. Others will take the plunge and make it from scratch with lye, oils, and a liquid. In either case, the operation is small and either for pleasure or low sales. The hobbyist will either stay a hobbyist or eventually start to move into one of the other classifications over time. The hobbyist soapmaker will generally produce income in the $500 to $5,000 range per year. There is nothing at all wrong with starting this way; most soapmakers do. If your goal is to become a hobbyist soapmaker and not start a business, you can skip the chapters to create a business and move right to the good stuff, making soap.

The Novelty soapmaker is someone who still has a day job but starts to contemplate the possibilities of turning their business into a full-time adventure. In addition to the hobbyist's activities, they will move out of the kitchen and into a dedicated space. This space might be within their home, a shared business space, or an external location. The novelty soapmaker will start experimenting with their own recipes and creations. They will register their business with the government; in some circumstances, they begin to collect and remit sales tax depending on total revenue. The novelty soapmaker will also join a soap guild and enroll in its business and product liability insurance program. They will start to pursue markets and sales channels outside of their circle of influence, possibly e-commerce and Etsy, local artisan and farmers markets, and local small retail locations. The novelty soapmaker will make larger batch productions and seek volume discounts on raw materials and packaging. They will start to professionalize their packaging and streamline their production methods. The novelty soapmaker will generally produce an income in the $2,500 to $30,000 range per year.

The functional soapmaker has generally gone through and expanded on the first two stages of hobbyist and novelty and is now getting serious about the business. They have or are moving into the business full time and giving up the old-day job. They have registered the business with the government, and they are collecting and remitting sales tax. The business is now in a dedicated space and flourishing. The functional soapmaker has expanded the product line to possibly include other natural skincare products like lip balms, hand, body, and face creams, deodorants, shampoos, shower gels, toothpaste, and more from their own formulations. They have created a registered brand and logo. They now sell on their website, third-party e-commerce platforms like Amazon, at all types of markets, in retail stores, and probably offer Private Label or White Label products to others. Some functional soapmakers will ultimately start a brick-and-mortar store, having their own retail space. They have a strong social media presence and have begun to do some advertising. The functional soapmaker has now hired a couple of employees. The business is growing. The functional soapmaker (Now Natural Skin Care Company) will generally produce an income in the $20,000 to six-figure plus range.

Where are you on this journey? Just a dream, starting at the hobbyist level or marching ahead as a functional skincare business. Independent of what stage you are at, this book will walk you through each step from conception to successful business and include everything in-between you will need to know and understand to get your product idea or passion to market and beyond. I will include tips and tricks and the dos and don'ts from experience gained through 15 years of research and five years of running a successful six-figure skincare business.

Consideration Two – What Type of Business Will You Start

The second consideration is to decide what type of business you will start. Each province, state, municipality, country, etc., all have their own rules and regulations around starting a business. It all depends on where you live and what type of business you want to create, provincial, state, or national. It would be impossible, and beyond this book's scope, to list the requirements for every location worldwide. In this area, you will have to do some homework seeking to understand your local regulation. We will discuss the types of business you can start and the implications of each type. Once you zero in on what type of business you want to start, you can educate yourself on that type where you live.

There are four main types of business structure or legal entities with different offshoots within them and called different things by different countries, states and provinces, but the premise is essentially the same. The four main types are sole proprietorship, partnership, limited liability company (LLC), and Corporations (Incorporated Companies). Each one is very different, so let's take a close look at them to help you decide.

The Sole Proprietorship

A sole proprietorship is the simplest form or least complex business type you can start. It is also by far the cheapest. The hobbyist usually begins with a sole proprietorship. Although requirements differ by area, you can register a sole proprietorship in your name or the business name of your choice in most locations. You can also self-register with the government avoiding the requirements to pay for a lawyer. If you choose a name for your business other than your own, you will need to conduct a name search to ensure that the name is not registered to someone else. Once you register, you will receive a business license number. Your income and expenses get added to your personal tax return at the end of each year. It only requires expense and income tracking. Once you hit a certain sales level, you might have to register for a sales tax account, charge, and remit sales tax. In some areas, you don't even need to register the business; you add the expenses and revenues to your personal tax return, and that's it. The sole proprietorship is also the most flexible and most straightforward business to make changes. It has the highest degree of control with no partner, officers, or board members to approve changes that you want to make. You are in full control. Check with your government authorities to understand what the jurisdictional requirements are where you live for sole proprietorships.

Although a sole proprietorship is the simplest and most flexible form of business you can start, it has drawbacks. You have unlimited liability, you are the business, and the business is you. Your personal property and wealth are attached to the business. It does not exist as a separate entity. If you run into financial trouble with the business, you are personally responsible for any debt the business has created. Lawsuits brought against the business are your responsibility to settle.

In most cases, as a sole proprietorship, finding outside capital or investors for your business is most likely not going to happen. You will be on your own to fund the business. Investors have a low comfort level lending to a business that is not a separate legal entity.

If you plan on growing your business into the functional stage, you will most likely want to incorporate it at this point. Although you can do it later, this will be a challenge. You will have to redo almost everything you have done to date, including but not limited to changing all of your packagings, labelling, stationery, advertising, and videos. You will have to adjust your website, third-party e-commerce sites, notify all suppliers, wholesalers, and customers, and so on to reflect your new legal entity.

The Partnership

The partnership is identical to the sole proprietorship in most ways except one. You have a partner or partners. As in a sole proprietorship, each partner is responsible for the company's liability and financial obligations. Each partner shares in the profits and reports income and expenses on their personal income tax.

Risks of partnerships also need to be taken into consideration when deciding to go down this road. Vision and direction need to be established and agreed to by all partners at the adventure's outset. Partners need to be flexible to each other's needs and business direction, helping avoid a stalemate in direction and growth. If this does not happen, rifts can develop within the partnership and threaten the business. Another problem is that if compensation is not in line with the business's individual contributions, partners can resent each other, threatening the business. It is important to know your partners well. It is advisable to have had a good prior personal or business relationship with your prospective partners. Know that partners are liable for their actions within the company and the actions of their partners.

The Limited Liability Company (LLC)

This form of company is not available in all countries. LLCs are becoming very popular where they are available. Check with your lawyer, local government, or regulatory body to see if this option is available. An LLC is essentially a hybrid of a sole proprietorship/partnership and a corporation. An LLC is an unincorporated entity. Income and expense flow through the individual(s) as in a sole proprietorship or partnership. Liability is limited to the amount of investment made into the company. Your personal assets are protected. Unlike a sole proprietorship, although you recognize income and expense personally and report these numbers on your personal tax return, they need to be kept separate and distinct as the LLC will need its own bank account and accounting system. Personal and business finances need to be kept separate and distinct. Taxation does not occur at the company level, like corporations. It occurs at a personal level, like sole proprietorships and partnerships.

Challenges of an LLC exist. In most locations, if a member dies, goes bankrupt, or leaves the company, the LLC will have to be dissolved and re-established by the remaining members. Also, members will need to contribute to the social security tax and medicare tax as self-employed income based on the companies total net earnings. Check with your lawyer, accountant, local government, or regulatory authority for LLC requirements if offered in your area.

The Corporation (Incorporated companies)

The corporation is a separate legal entity from you. It is its own entity. To look at it another way, it is its own person. It can buy, sell, borrow money, sue, and be sued just like people can. Generally, a corporation or an incorporated company protects your personal assets from judgments and lawsuits. The corporation bears the brunt of exposure from creditors and legal action against it, not you personally. Your only exposure is generally only to the extent of your investment in the company. The exception to this, if you engage in illegal activity or break the law on behalf of the corporation. Corporations are owned by shareholders and run by directors. Shareholders can also be directors and usually are unless it is a public or large company. The majority of shareholders do not work for the company; they invest in it for profit. I won't be discussing public companies here as they do not apply to this book. If you have a company you are taking public, you are beyond the scope of this book and congratulations. (Chuckle).

It costs a little more to start a corporation as this is usually done for you by a lawyer. When you register your corporation, you will decide on a name and have it searched for availability. If available, you will register that name, and you should trademark it. A lawyer generally performs registration of the corporation, name, and trademark registration for you. I have seen companies incorporated for $500 up to $2,500 for startups. If you decide to go the incorporation route, find a good, reasonably priced lawyer to get your company incorporated. Seek advice from an accountant on how to best internally structure the shares for your best tax advantages. The share structure and classification will depend on your personal circumstances when you begin, and your accountant can advise you.

Once you establish your corporation, you will receive a company seal and a registrar to keep your articles of incorporation. This seal is used to recognize the company when performing such actions as opening a bank account or dealing with legal papers or contracts. The articles of incorporation will include, as an example, who the shareholders are, and how many shares are issued. It will also have the corporation's address, the signing authorities, the directors and how long they will serve, when your fiscal year-end is, sometime throughout the year, or at the calendar year-end. It will contain the bylaws that you have established and the rules around changing those bylaws. It will contain the minutes of your Board of directors' meetings. The Board will need to meet at a minimum of once per year. If this all sounds complicated, it isn't. Your lawyer will walk you through each step and do most of the grunt work to get up and running.

The advantages of a corporation are numerous. Personal assets are generally protected; it will be much easier to raise money. A corporation can access capital from many sources. Adding a legal suffix behind your corporation's name like Inc. or Incorporated brings instant legitimacy and authority to the business. Corporate profits are taxed at a lower tax rate than personal income. Shareholders can receive compensation from the corporation in dividends that carry a lower tax rate than employment income. Employees can be issued stock options to help with retention and establish a motivated workforce. The corporate entity exists beyond the exit or death of a shareholder. Branding and recognition begin at the inception of the company. When your corporation is large enough, you can take the company public if this is your goal.

Corporations do come with some disadvantages. You will have some legal and accounting fees each year. You can reduce these by doing as much of the work on your own that you can. If you do not have the skills, learn them. We are going to look at some of the required skills as we go through the chapters. Corporations require more recordkeeping and reporting than other forms of business.

Summary

Before you start your business or spend your first dollar, it is paramount that you take these two considerations to heart. Deciding what type of soapmaker you aspire to be and what kind of business you want to start will make your life so much easier as you go through this journey. If you are having trouble deciding, seek assistance and recommendations from an accountant or lawyer. Speak with other small business owners who have achieved success and garner help and opinions from them based on the experiences they have gone through.

Recommendations

When my wife Fonda and I started LifeGevity Soap Company Inc. in 2016, we incorporated with each of us, becoming shareholders and directors on day one. We knew we would become full-time soapmakers, we knew we would grow and expand the business quickly, and we knew we ultimately wanted to start a corporation. We didn't want to go through the hassle of making the changes to become a corporation a year down the road; this would have been a tremendous amount of work. The little bit of extra expense at the outset to form the corporation was well worth it. If we had to do it over, we would not change a thing.

If you are still unsure at this point about what type of soapmaker you want to be or want to experiment a little to see if it is the right fit for you. Or, if you know that you will never take your business past the hobbyist level, I would recommend starting a sole proprietorship or partnership if applicable.

If you are certain this business is for you, you have decided to unwaveringly follow your dream, start a corporation for all the benefits it brings. I have always seen LLCs as having one foot in and one foot out. If starting a soapmaking business is what you want to do, take the plunge. If you decide to change your direction down the road, you can sell the corporation, put it into a dormant state, or shut it down. Take the time to work through your decision. Seek the advice of a lawyer and accountant. With all of that said, start now, take action now. The business is not going to create itself. Dreams only become a reality if you make them happen.

Happy soaping!

STARTING A SUCCESSFUL BUSINESS
Do You Have What it Takes

"The world needs dreamers and the world needs doers. But above all, the world needs dreamers who do."
—Sarah Ban Breathnach

MANY PEOPLE DREAM OF STARTING A BUSINESS. Very few do it. Why is that? Some never get there because of fear, others because of a lack of confidence. People often tell me they have not started their business because of a perception of a lack of resources or money. There are many reasons why people claim they do not start. I don't accept any of these reasons. I believe most people don't start their business because they don't know how to start. They have not put in the time, research, and effort to move past their hurdles and get on with things. Anything in life can be scary; the unknown usually is. Anything in life can also be accomplished. I firmly believe that. No one has ever said it would be easy, and if they have, they have probably never started a business. As they say, no risk, no reward. If you are confident in your product or service, in our case, soapmaking, and are prepared to roll up your sleeves and get dirty with some hard work, you can do it. Period. This book will teach you how. The real trick is not just to do it but to do it successfully.

Most new businesses fail. It is a simple fact. Although you can find different statistics, the general consensus is up to 70% of new businesses fail within the first year. Only 20% of new businesses make it to their 5th year. You can find statistics that move these percentages 10% either way. It is concerning. In my study and analysis over the years, I have observed common traits in businesses that have failed and common traits in businesses that have succeeded. There are very specific reasons for both. If you want to be successful in your new venture and be one of the 20% who succeeds, there are steps you need to take, sacrifices you will need to make. I don't say this to scare you. I say it to prepare you for your success. If you can answer yes to the majority of the following, you are well on your way. If you cant answer yes, you should probably keep your day job until you can.

Hard work. Yes, most books you read or videos you watch on starting a business will tell you to work hard, and they are right. What they don't usually tell you is how to work hard. You do need to work hard, or better phrased, work smart while working hard. If you are reading a book that tells you that you only have to work smart and not hard, throw that book out. You are being duped. If you are prepared to put in some hard work and to work smart, check the box.

Education. Yes, you will need to educate yourself and increase your knowledge in many new areas that you might not be familiar with today. Most new entrepreneurs cannot hire professional services for every area of their business they need help with on day one. In most cases, it is going to be up to you. If you are prepared to educate yourself in new areas you know little or nothing about, check the box.

Skills. Yes, skills. Education instills knowledge and wisdom. Skills are practical application and functional, where the rubber hits the road, so to speak. You will need to gain new skills in many areas to achieve success in your business. If you don't know how to accomplish a specific task, you will have to acquire the skill to get it done. If you are prepared to learn new skills, check the box.

Comfort zone. Yes, your comfort zone. You will have to involve yourself in areas you are either uncomfortable with or have no experience; maybe it is sales, accounting, production, graphic arts, regulations, advertising, etc. You will need to be able to move outside of your comfort zone to get some things accomplished. If you are prepared to step outside of your comfort zone, check the box.

Exceptional, Yes, you need to be exceptional in all that you do or make. The biggest reason for businesses failing is mediocrity. You can find thousands of mediocre soapmaking businesses out there that flounder through the months, making a part-time wage at best. There are only a couple of exceptional ones. If you want to achieve success and rise above the pack, you have to distinguish yourself as being the best of the best. Both you and your business need to be exceptional. Your product or service needs to be exceptional. If you are prepared to be exceptional, check the box.

Customer service, yes, your bread and butter, the customer. If you read through the reviews most businesses receive, both large and small, what is the primary complaint? It is always first, customer service, and second, inferior products or services. Today's customer is tired of autoboots, elevator music, being left on hold, rude customer service people, tired of being belittled, being passed around, or brushed off. Today's customer is tired of not having their issues resolved and is tired of buying inferior products and cheap products. If you are prepared to create both an exceptional customer service experience and an exceptional product, check the box.

Flexibility, yes, flexibility. You are going to make a plan for your business. Life is going to happen, and make its own plan throwing yours out the window. Learning to make many adjustments along the way, both big and small, as you learn and grow in your new adventure will be paramount to your success. If you can be flexible and accept change as it comes, check the box.

Discernment, yes, discernment. In today's information and technology age, anyone and everyone is here to offer advice and tell you how to get rich or be successful. There are no get-rich-quick schemes that are legal, and if you are listening to someone who tells you there are, turn them off. You have been duped. With the internet and social media, you have at your fingertips more information available today than at any time in our history. The problem is, not all, but the majority of what you will read or study on these platforms is pure garbage and will lead you down the rabbit hole. If you are prepared to diligently spend time discerning between what is valuable and what is garbage, check the box.

So, do you have what it takes to start a successful soapmaking business? If you were able to check the box on the majority of the above items, you most likely do. It is time to either get started or take your business to the next level. The following chapters will first walk you through each of the areas above. We will then move into the specifics of how to start or expand your soapmaking business, including how to make soap, ingredients, recipes, production tools and machinery, production methods, labelling, packaging, graphic arts, regulations, record keeping, accounting, sales, marketing, advertising, and distribution. We will conclude with how to expand your business and take the next steps to greater success.

Happy soaping.

THE TOOLS OF SUCCESS
Preparing Yourself For Your Journey

"The expectations of life depend upon diligence; the mechanic that would perfect his work must first sharpen his tools."
—Confucius

MOST NEW BUSINESS OWNERS will tell you that after a long day's work, they only made a couple of dollars per hour, and yes, this is the reality of starting a new business. They will tell you that there are not enough hours in the day, yes, also a reality of starting a new business. When starting out, you are going to have to be prepared to work long hours every day. The time will come when you can sit back, have employees do the work, and collect your money. Starting out is not that time. Accept that your days will be long. With a little training and working smart, these long days will be a joy rather than a chore. If you enjoy what you are doing and take pride in what you are creating, you will never work another day in your life. If you are doing what you love and love what you are doing, your days will be filled with your passions and spent fulfilling your dreams. Your head will hit the pillow at night wishing the next day was already here to get back to your adventure.

Work Hard, Work Smart

When starting a business, time is your greatest asset and your greatest enemy. Learn not to waste it, the first step to success. Don't try to recreate the wheel or develop something from scratch that is readily available to you. This is a time-waster. For example, why spend one week developing the perfect test mold for your first test batch of soap when you can use an empty cleaned-out milk carton. Why spend hours calculating saponification rates for different oils when saponification charts are a readily available resource from soapmaking supply companies and so on. Use your time wisely, as once an hour has gone by, you can never get it back.

As they say, measure twice, cut once. Ensure that you understand the task at hand before tackling it. Have a recipe printed out, make sure your ingredients are available and pre-measured, ensure your batteries in your scale are fresh, make sure your thermometer has been calibrated, and so on. If you spend too much time fixing errors or delaying the completion of a task because of poor preparation rather than accomplishing the task at hand, you are wasting time.

Don't be a shuffler. Shuffling is one of the worst time-wasters in your day. If you pick up a piece of paper, deal with it. Don't put it in a pile for later. Once finished with an item, put it away. Have a place for everything and make sure everything is in its place. Why spend time looking for an item that is not where it should be, another time waster. Or why spend time moving items from here to there, more wasted time. If you spend a little time analyzing how much time in a day you waste shuffling items from here to there, you will be amazed. Work smart and recapture this time for task completion and to get things accomplished.

Concentrate on your task at hand. Having ten tasks going at once is an inefficient use of your time. If you are designing a label, design a label. If you are making soap, make soap. If you are managing a web page, manage the webpage. You efficiently complete tasks when you concentrate on one at a time. You will find more value in completing one task in its entirety with perfection rather than completing a small piece of ten tasks.

Remove distractions. Turn the TV off, send the pets outside, create a secure and dedicated space to work, set the phone aside, the text or email can wait. Distractions promote errors. Errors are time wasters. Why spend time fixing an error or possibly losing a whole batch of soap because you were watching the TV to see why Sally was breaking up with Johhny. Soapmaking is an exacting science and needs your full attention and intense focus.

Set a daily schedule and task list. Don't flutter here and there. When creating your get things done today list, set the order of completion by prioritizing the tasks. If you are a more artistic person that does not do well with lists and schedules, see the section above on learning new skills.

Schedules and to-do lists create a sense of importance and urgency. They help you to get going and give you direction.

Last but not least, work to your biological clock. Hmm, what does that mean? If you are a morning person, plan your important and prioritized tasks in the morning. If you are a night person, schedule your important and prioritized tasks in the evening. The corporate world has conditioned us to the 9 to 5 routine. Now that you are your own boss, you make the rules. If you are an evening person, why get up at 6 am to make soap when your body is not waking up and functioning efficiently until 10 am. This makes no sense. Work when you work best, you will be more productive and prone to fewer mistakes.

Education

As a new business owner, you will need to educate yourself in areas you probably know little about or in areas that are outside of your comfort zone. For most, this is the scariest thing about starting a business. It is also the easiest to accomplish with a little planning and preparation. Education is not just for the young; it should be a lifelong pursuit. Learning new things keeps your mind sharp, and some might argue, your body young. Here are some tips. Start a binder with tabbed sections. Each time you run into an area that you know nothing or little about, create a tab for this area in the binder. We will call it an educational resource binder. It can be physical or electronic. I use tabbed sheets in excel saved in a file I call Educational Resources.

Once you have recognized an area of weakness, get to work. Start studying everything of value, and I highlight "of value" on the subject. As you research and educate yourself, keep a copy of each resource that has value in your binder or electronic file for future reference. Some items might be a text or photocopy of an educational article, the internet address, or a link to your studying resource. It can be an excerpt from a book or a white paper on the subject. Maybe it is a copy of the government labelling guidelines and so on. By building this resource of collected educational materials for yourself, you do two things. First, you have an area to house articles and items you have deemed important and valuable while eliminating junk. Second, you have created a reference binder that you can refer back to as required. You will most likely be unable to memorize everything you are learning, so you are leaving yourself a resource you can easily refer back to as needed without having to research the same stuff over and over continually.

Each of us learns in different ways. If the printed Word is your preferred avenue of learning, seek written resources. If you are a visual learner, seek out videos you can bookmark and refer to as required. If taking a course is how you learn best, take a course. You are in control to educate yourself in ways that work for you. Keeping your educational resource binder makes it simple to expand your knowledge base and have your continuing educational resources available at your fingertips. If you are not a structured person, start learning this new skill.

Skills

You will most likely be learning new skills almost every day as you embark on your new adventure. Education is knowledge. Skills are practical applications where the rubber meets the road, so to speak. When you educate yourself, you are absorbing new information. When you learn a new skill, you are physically completing a task that you were unable to complete before, or at least not very well. For example, have you created a spreadsheet, created a label in a graphics art program, made soap with the cold or hot process method, experimented with creating your own unique recipes, met with a supplier to negotiate a price and payment terms? If not, you are going to need to learn how to accomplish these tasks and many more. Although daunting for some, this is where the fun begins because you get to start to touch and feel stuff. You now get to be creative and let the creative juices flow.

The only way to effectively learn a new skill is to dig right in and get your hands dirty. This is one of the areas where you will make mistakes and mess stuff up. That is absolutely fine and part of the learning process and, I might add, part of the fun. No one learns to ride a bike without falling on their butt a couple of times. If you mess something up, know what went wrong and try again. Keep on trying and learning until you get it right. Sometimes it is a process of trial and error. Sometimes it is a process of making equipment or recipe adjustments. Sometimes you will need to review and study your learning resources. Other times you might have to retrace steps and troubleshoot because you don't have a clue what went sideways.

You might have to repeat a skill you are learning over and over to become proficient at it. When I first started trimming soap by hand, the finished bars looked like something a two-year-old carved out. Today after years of experience, I can trim a bar of soap blindfolded in the dark in one-tenth of the time it used to take me, and the bars look great. Learning a new skill takes patience, practice, and time, and this is just fine. You will get out what you put in. Effort, patience, and having endurance equal reward in this area. As you tackle new skill learning, dig in, get dirty, and have fun. It is part of the experience.

Comfort Zone

In my many years of experience as a senior corporate executive, in almost all cases, if someone is not comfortable with a task assigned to them, they exhibit one main characteristic - procrastination. Procrastination can come in many forms. I believe people procrastinate for two main reasons: they fall into the lazy category or the fear of failure category. Since you desire to start a business, I will assume you do not fall into the lazy category. Fear of failure promotes procrastination in people in a couple of different ways. The first and most obvious is a reluctance to get the task started. The second is to doodle through the job chasing every distraction they can find to avoid the continuing pain of working outside their comfort zone. Procrastination is your enemy and needs to be defeated. Here are some tips and tricks to help you be productive in areas that you are not comfortable.

Start by recognizing and accepting this is a challenging area for you. Once you confess to yourself and acknowledge that you are outside of your comfort zone, you can now prepare to tackle what you face head-on in a little different manner than the easy tasks you march through. To be successful in getting through areas outside of your comfort zone, you need to start by redefining what comfort is. Have you not done it before? Do you think you are not good at it? Are you afraid of getting it wrong? So what and who cares. Treat it as a new exciting adventure. Treat it as something you are determined to get the best of rather than letting it get the best of you. Start by changing your mindset.

When you sit down to enjoy a nice meal, you don't pick your plate up and dump it into your mouth and swallow it in one big gulp. You take little bites, spending time enjoying the textures and flavours as you slowly enjoy and eat your meal. Treat tasks that are outside of your comfort zone in this same way, like a good meal. Break the task into little bites and tackle those small bites one by one until you have completed the whole. How do you eat an elephant? One bite at a time, as they say. (I am not advocating the eating of elephants; it's a metaphor, chuckle. Some readers have taken this literally.)

Use all the possible tools at your disposal to get through areas of discomfort. If you are making your first sales call and are not comfortable doing this, take someone with you - someone with experience who is good with sales. If you need to create a costing sheet but are not comfortable with spreadsheets, consult your educational resource binder. If this item has not yet made your binder, get to the task of educating yourself with spreadsheets adding this resource material to your binder.

You can have someone with experience walk you through a spreadsheet program, watch some YouTube instructional videos, open up your spreadsheet program, start playing around in it to get familiar with its functionality, etc. The most important thing is to do it. Roll up your sleeves and get busy learning. Don't let it beat you, don't give up. Keep trying until you get it.

Designate a reward for yourself for the completion of the task. A glass of wine, a piece of Belgian chocolate, a scented bubble bath, a trip to the spa, a meal at your favourite restaurant, tickets to the big game, whatever makes you happy. Once you complete the task, take the reward.

Don't put off until later what you can do right now. The task is most likely not going to go away. The longer you put it off, the more daunting it will become, and the more stress you will create for yourself through the period of procrastination. Put the above tips into action and just get it done.

Exceptional

The simple fact is, there are a lot of artisan natural soapmakers out there. Most, at best, are small mediocre businesses that will never amount to much. If you are going to enter the soapmaking business, you will need to be one of the best to make any headway. Competition should never scare you. It should motivate you to rise above the pack, to be the best at what you do. You need to have exceptional customer service, a superior product, an exceptional sales and marketing program, remarkable product displays, and so on. You will need to demonstrate that you are the definitive authority, the most knowledgeable, the best prepared to deliver the experience and product today's customer demands. At the onset of your business, set your mental attitude to achieve excellence. Settle for nothing mediocre. Be mediocre, and you will be just another one of the hundreds of soapmakers out there slogging through each day, not accomplishing very much. Be the best, and you can't fail. Set your sights on excellence, design everything you do to achieve greatness, and you will achieve great success. Your business will grow quicker than your grandest expectations.

Customer Service

No customers, no business. Period. Your sole objective in all you do is to gain loyal customers. Once you gain a new customer, how do you turn that customer into a loyal repeat customer who promotes your products with family, friends, and coworkers? One who gives you 5-star reviews? Customer service is the answer!

Getting new customers is 5 to 7 times harder than keeping current customers. Loyal repeat customers are like gold. Once you get them, you need to keep them. You accomplish this by first, of course, having a great product and excellent service. Customers will want to know why your soap is better than the next booth over. Being knowledgeable about your product and how you make it is your opportunity to shine with your customers. Your customers will be mesmerized as you teach them how you handcraft your soap and what natural ingredients you use. They will want to hear about the pure essential oils you use and what the therapeutic benefits are. Your customers will be fascinated with your story of how you lovingly handcraft each bar and will be excited to get some home to try.

The next step is to give your customers the absolute best customer service experience they have ever received. When they call you, answer the phone, call back within two hours if you miss the call. When they email or text, respond right away. If you are unable to do so, respond within half an hour. If they have an issue, settle it without complaint or delay. Most customers understand that problems will arise. Customers who have had an issue resolved to exceed their expectations become more loyal than customers who have not. The customer will score you on how well and how quickly you settle their matter. When you are seeing a customer face to face, smile, be pleasant, be polite. When you are talking to a customer on the phone, smile, be friendly, be respectful.

Here is a real-world example of a customer complaint that I had to deal with and the result. We sold a couple of our all-natural lemon soap bars to an elderly lady at one of our weekly artisan markets. We were caught off-guard when she returned the following week to complain. Her complaint was our soap bars were too big to fit into her hands. Chuckle. Rather than having a good laugh, my first thought, I took a bar of our sweet orange soap and cut it in half. I then bagged the two half bars up with some tissue paper and gave them to her with our compliments – no fee. I told her each week she comes, I will cut her bars in half, and it will be like getting two bars rather than one. She left with the biggest smile you can imagine, and to this day, five years later, she continues to be a loyal customer purchasing both our lemon and orange soaps. The moral of this true story – every customer complaint should end in a satisfied repeat customer. There are no rules against creativity, only solutions to satisfying the customer and gaining their loyalty.

When dealing with customers, make them feel special, go the extra mile, show them they are important to you. Show them appreciation. Thank them for their business every chance you get!

Flexibility

I would be considered an inflexible person. I am very structured. I eat the same breakfast every morning, set a schedule for my day, and keep the same regiment as closely as possible. How boring, right? When I do the dishes, I line the big plates up one by one like soldiers in a row. The small plates come next, equidistant and parallel to the big plates and so on - structure. Making a change in my routine is tough for me. It does not come naturally.

On the other hand, my wife and business partner Fonda, is the complete opposite. She is a free spirit chasing after every shiny object she sees, fluttering here and there as the wind blows. When she stacks dishes in the drainboard, it is like a train wreck. I have to look away. Dishes are thrown in every direction, with no order, no structure. It's horrible. I get the shudders just thinking about it. Chuckle. Sticking to a routine or having structure does not come naturally to Fonda.

The problem is, neither state, being inflexible, or having too much flexibility, are successful traits when starting a business. You need to find a balance somewhere right near the middle. Events are going to happen that throw your schedule out the window — a power failure, a broken tool, a customer emergency, a snowstorm, etc. You require discipline in certain areas. Soapmaking is a precise science with ingredients measured to the 10th of a gram. Cooking and mixing temperatures need to be exact. The customer deadline will need to be achieved, etc. These are not flexible events. Finding a balance is very hard if you lean in either direction. But it has to be done. Striking a balance between these two states was one of the most challenging areas for Fonda and me. However, we both recognize the requirement to make the necessary adjustments and work daily to achieve those adjustments. It was not easy, and it won't be easy for you if you are of extremes like us.

The best advice I can give you is to make adjustments and accept those adjustments as part of your formula for success. The flexible needs to become a little more inflexible. The inflexible needs to become a bit more flexible. Keep a positive attitude. Grumbling or being upset is not going to help you or anyone else. Consider striking this even balance as a new skill set, making you a better, more productive, and well-rounded person.

Discernment

I spent ten years reading every book, blog, and article I could find on soapmaking before making my first bar of soap. I am a bit of a researcher. 90% of these resources were junk filled with incorrect information, incomplete information, wrong information, and sometimes dangerous information. As an example, Canadian labelling laws require you to list the International Nomenclature of Cosmetic Ingredients. (INCI) for your ingredients list on each of your labels. Each country has its own rules. We will address this in the labelling chapter. The majority of the books tell you to list the botanical names for ingredients or just the English names like Olive Oil. This is bad advice for anyone in Canada and some of the other countries. This advice could also lead to some hefty fines for non-compliance. Incorrect labelling can get you into trouble with the government. Each country has its own regulations. I watched a person on YouTube teaching soapmaking pour a batch of unsaponified soap batter into a mould with large chunks of unmixed or raw lye into a curing mould. Shudder—two examples of hundreds I could give you.

You should exercise caution when choosing your learning resources. I always ask myself, 'Who wrote the book, what makes them qualified, and what makes them the subject matter expert'? Then, I dig in and do my research on the educator. Do they have any actual valid experience? Have they been successful? Can I find credible, positive reviews on their work? Is their teaching relative to what I am trying to learn and accomplish? In our case, have they actually started, and do they run, or have they run a successful soapmaking business? If you cannot answer these questions, don't buy the book or continue reading their blog. They are not actual experts. You are being duped.

Today, we run into problems with the advent of self-publishing and the internet freely available for anyone to create what they want. With many people's desire to get rich quickly with blogging, writing, and creating YouTube videos, there is a plethora of misinformation, wrong information, incomplete information, and sometimes downright dangerous information. It is going to be up to you to discern what is valuable and what is not. If it sounds too good to be true, it probably is. It probably isn't sensible or reasonable if it does not make a lot of sense or pass the reasonableness test. If you are being told you can get rich in a week following this 'proven method' run! Spend your time seeking out qualified people that can demonstrate a record of success — those who have exceptional reviews and are clearly top of their class. You will save an incredible amount of time and effort with a little study out of the gate. There are great educators out there, but you will need to put in a little effort to find them. Avoid being led down the rabbit hole and wasting your time. Valuable time that you can never get back.

Business Plan

To start a business, you need a plan. You can't just wake up and start doing stuff. Well, you can, but you won't get very far. You need a plan, a template, a direction to follow, where you are going, and how you plan to get there. A business plan can be simple or mind-boggling complex. Somewhere in between is what you want.

There are literally thousands of free business plan tutorials and template resources available online, so I will not dive too deeply into this area. You can even find one in the Microsoft word templates. Find a suitable template from a reputable source and start creating your plan. Most of these resources are free.

A business plan is a fluid document, meaning that you adjust your plan as you make adjustments to your business. You can create your plan in a spreadsheet program like Excel or a word processing program like Word, or a PowerPoint presentation program. You can, of course, use your preferred equivalent. I personally prefer spreadsheet programs rather than embedding spreadsheets into a word or presentation document. I can create spreadsheets right in the plan. The most popular method for creating a business plan is within presentation programs like PowerPoint or its equivalents. Although considered 'Old School,' you can even create your plan with pen and paper.

Write your business plan as if your intended audience knows nothing about your business. Your business plan should leave your audience with a clear understanding of your business, where it is going, how it will get there, and how fast. Its intended purpose is not only to give you a template to follow and adjust as you go. Your business plan is also created for external audiences like your banker or potential investors. You will need a detailed business plan if you intend to borrow money for your business in the future.

A business plan, at a minimum, should include the mission or vision statement of the company. It should consist of a section on you and the other owners and key stakeholders if you have partners. Include a description of your company and its products or services. Describe how your company will be distinct from your competition and who that competition is. Your intended markets and how you plan to reach those markets should be listed. Touch on production, sales, and revenue projections. You will also want to include five-year growth projections and finish with a conclusion.

Creating a business plan might sound like a daunting task. It is not. If you have come this far, you are serious about your business. You already have a good idea about each of the elements of your plan. Creating a business plan formalizes those elements in print, giving you a template to follow. Don't skip this step!

Moving Foreward

If any of the above topics have raised an eyebrow or caused you consternation, you should spend some time contemplating what steps you need to take to become comfortable tackling your new adventure. Spend some time looking at other learning resources. Spend some time talking to others who have travelled this journey. I believe you will find this chapter to be sound advice and an excellent springboard to get you going.

If you cannot wrap your head around the areas listed above, you might not be ready to jump into a business just yet. If this is the case, this is ok. It is better to be prepared to achieve success than be unprepared and fail. If you are ready to embrace each of these areas listed above, you are ready to go. You are well on your way to starting and running a successful business, so let's get started. Read on.

GETTING STARTED
Location Location Location

YOU ARE MOST LIKELY EITHER DABBLING IN SOAPMAKING or just getting ready to start. Either way, it is decision time. Where are you going to set up your operation? Almost every new soapmaker begins in the kitchen. Although easy, practical, and you can start right now, it is not a good plan. Many people will tell you this is ok. I'm afraid I have to disagree and recommend you don't do this for the following reasons.

First off, to make real natural soap, you will need to use either sodium hydroxide (lye), for bar soap, or potassium hydroxide (potash), for liquid soap. These are caustic chemicals, and you do not want them anywhere near your food preparation surfaces. You do not need to be scared of these chemicals. When handled properly and safely, there is no issue with these items. They simply don't belong in the kitchen. People tell me no, no, Brian, I wear my safety gear, and I am cautious. You might think this is the case; however, when using a stick blender or transferring your hydroxide solution to mixing pots, you have no control where the micro spay from the blender or drips from the measuring cup are landing. I guarantee you I can go into any kitchen making soap and find traces of caustic lye.

Secondly, you never want to use a pot, utensil, or measuring cup to cook your food that has come into contact with soapmaking. It is not worth the risk. You need to segregate all of your soap-making equipment from your food-making equipment. Here is where the problem comes in. Our natural tendencies are to take the easy road. Suppose you forget to bring a dedicated utensil or measuring cup or whatever to the kitchen for your soapmaking. In that case, you will most likely grab the closest item available, which just happens to be an item you use to make food. An imperfect plan, but I have seen it happen in almost every case I have witnessed.

The third issue, your kitchen is most likely one of the busiest rooms in the house with the most traffic. Drinks from the fridge, snacks from the cupboard, dropping dishes off, the hang-out, etc. We talked about the need to work in a distraction-free environment for many reasons. The kitchen is not it. If you are a pet or kid owner, the soapmaking environment is absolutely not for them. Both curious creatures, you only have to be distracted once, and tragedy can happen. I am sure you don't want any part of that.

The fourth issue is perception, the perception of both yourself and your potential customers. There is nothing more detrimental to your growth and success than not projecting an image of professionalism. When a customer asks you where you produce your products, and you tell them your kitchen, in most cases, blow that potential customer a kiss goodbye as they leave. Your chance of seeing them again is slim. You also need to remove yourself from the kitchen for your own esteem. Making soap in your kitchen will not give you a feeling of accomplishment. You will not feel that you are starting and running a successful business that makes you feel proud.

The fifth issue will affect some, but not all. There are a significant number of people starting home-based businesses today. Unfortunately, you need to consider government regulations and bylaws. Creating an office in your home in an urban residential area is usually not a problem. Running a thriving manufacturing plant in your home is almost always a no-no in an urban residential neighbourhood. Some bylaws and regulations will allow artisan crafting up to a certain amount of annual revenue in your home.

If you own a farm or a rural property, there is generally no issue. This is one of those areas where you will have to do some homework, and what you learn will depend on where you live geographically, how your property is zoned, and what your local bylaws and government regulations are. Most new soapmakers start in their home, ignore the regulations, and never get 'Caught.' If you want to do this properly, do your homework. It might not be worth the risk or the consequences if you ignore the rules and get caught. If you find out you can not legally do this in your home, you will have to find a small business place to rent. You can also find small shared spaces in most locations reasonably priced.

You will also need to contact your insurance company and let them know you are now running a business from your home. Most insurance companies will increase your premiums to cover the increased risk if they allow the activity. If they don't, you might have to find a new insurance company. If you do not inform your insurance company, you are running a business from your home; you run the risk of not receiving a payout if you need to make an insurance claim. I know the zoning, bylaw, and insurance issues are a pain, and most of us don't want to deal with it, but unfortunately, they are part of the gig when starting a business independent of it being in the home or in a rented space.

So, where does that leave you? You might run a business from your home and choose to use your kitchen. The biggest thing I hear is, "I don't have a choice." Ah, but you do. If something is important to us, we figure it out. Make this important to you, and you will figure it out. I understand the need to save costs in the early days, and most new soapmakers cannot run out and start renting manufacturing space. We were all there at one point. It does not mean you can't make some minor adjustments here and there to solve or eliminate the above issues and obstacles.

Do you have a garage, a room seldom used, a room full of collected junk, a basement, or an outbuilding. Most of us can create a dedicated space somewhere in our home to call our own to make private from the distractions and dangers listed above. Clear a spot out and make it secure from pets and children by putting a lock on the door. Voila, you now have an instant dedicated soap studio. Now that sounds impressive. When a customer asks where you make your soap, you can now tell them, in my soap studio. Now they are impressed! Once you add some stainless steel production tables, some shelves, your soapmaking equipment, and raw materials, you are all set to start making soap (All coming up in subsequent chapters).

If you do not have a dedicated water supply, the best answer is to install one. If you are unable to, you can bring jugs of water to your studio. You can clean your soaping dishes and utensils in the laundry tub or a water pail. You will need a container for transport. This is not an issue. I will teach you how to neutralize any lye deposits before transport.

Once you have a dedicated space ready to go, you are one step closer to getting your business up and running.   After we look at the science of soap, we will look at setting up your soap studio to start production.

THE SCIENCE OF SOAP
Natural VS Synthetic

"Nothing in life is to be feared, it is only to be understood. Now is the time to understand more, so that we may fear less."
—Marie Curie

WE ARE GOING TO TAKE A QUICK DETOUR from our discussion on getting set up with our production area and setting that production area up to look at what natural means, the different types of soap, and the science of soap, and the various production methods. We need to take this detour. To set up your soap studio with equipment and tools, you need to determine what production method or methods you will be using.

When you head into your local grocery or drugstore to buy conventional soap, you are not buying actual soap in most cases. You are buying detergent — a cocktail of synthetics, more often than not, toxic chemicals designed to mimic soap. Most conventional soap contains parabens, sodium lauryl sulphate (SLS), coal tars, and many more synthetics and toxins. Parabens are synthetic preservatives, SLS is a synthetic foaming agent, the same stuff they make pesticides out of, coal tars are a known carcinogen. In a subsequent chapter, we will discuss ingredients, the good, the bad, and the ugly. The large corporations figured out it is cheaper to make and sell you a cocktail of toxic synthetics than a natural bar or bottle of soap.

As people are becoming more educated about the dangers of these synthetics and toxins, they have started moving towards natural alternatives in droves, opening up the opportunity for aspiring natural soapmakers to enter into this business. It is estimated the soap business is a 25 billion dollar industry in North America alone and growing at a rate of 5% per year, not including all the other natural skincare products you can produce. With people moving to natural products, it is a great time to start your natural soapmaking business.

So what is natural? Defining what is natural has become very contentious in the industry. Most governments have not regulated the definition of natural, leaving the industry to regulate itself. Allowing large conglomerates to self-regulate or even the industry, in general, has created an atmosphere of confusion and, in my opinion, dishonesty. People who choose all-natural products want just that, all-natural products, not some natural and synthetic hybrid. Many large corporations are jumping on the natural bandwagon because they have recognized the industry trend to move to natural products. The corporations want their piece of the pie. They produce pretty packaging with green leaves on them, scenes of lavender fields, and use the Word natural.

Adding a couple of natural ingredients to a cocktail of synthetics and toxins does not make a product natural. I would boycott any product sold as natural that has synthetics in it, period. The second thing to watch for is the large corporations buying out successful natural product companies, then changing the ingredients and packaging but still selling it as natural. A couple of good examples to look at would be Burt's Bees or Toms of Maine. There are many more examples. A little research into these two companies will surprise you. Take a look at the ingredients lists or packaging before being bought by the large corporations compared to today.

The good news, today's natural product consumer has become wise to the corporate games and has become very good at checking label ingredients. Reviewing and understanding the ingredients listed on the label is our defence against being duped by corporations. Our biggest job as artisan soapmakers is to educate our consumers and teach them to read and understand labels.

Your first job is to determine your definition of safe and natural and then stick to it and be prepared to defend it. Almost all-natural raw materials, essential oils, carrier oils, clays, salts, milk, etc., go through an extraction process. One way to produce an essential oil is steam distillation, and another is compression, as two examples. As long as there are no synthetics added to essential oils, most consider them natural products. So there is a starting point for us to define what we consider natural.

My definition of natural is a product derived from only a natural source with no synthetics or artificial ingredients added. I will only use raw ingredients considered safe by independent reporting companies like EWG when it comes to safety. Just because an ingredient fits a natural definition does not mean it is safe to apply to the skin. An example would be formaldehyde, a product you will find in a lot of skincare formulas. Formaldehyde is a naturally occurring substance derived from carbon, hydrogen, and oxygen. The government will tell you it is safe up to a specific usage percentage. No thank you! The EPA has classified formaldehyde as a "probable human carcinogen."! EWG's SkinDeep scores formaldehyde 8-10, with 10 being the highest risk they assign.

You should eliminate or not use any ingredient that has any controversy or health risk attached to it. You should only use ingredients derived from nature with no added synthetics, ingredients that are not human-made. If you follow these two guidelines, you should have no issue labelling and selling your products as all-natural. You can defend your definition of natural, and you will be able to sleep well at night, knowing you are not trying to pull the wool over your customer's heads. I believe governments will eventually regulate the term natural. When this does happen, you will be well-positioned and most likely not be required to make too many, if any, changes to your recipes, ingredients lists, and labels.

The Science of Soap

Natural soap can only be created with an alkali, a fat or vegetable fatty acid, and a liquid. The alkali we use is either sodium hydroxide (lye) or potassium hydroxide (potash). Natural soap, be it bar, liquid, or cream, is produced with these three ingredients. To make bar soap, we use sodium hydroxide (lye). To make liquid soap, we use potassium hydroxide (Potash). To make cream soap, we use either sodium hydroxide, potassium hydroxide, or a combination of both.

The second required ingredient is animal fat or fatty acid derived from vegetables, fruits, or nuts. From this point forward, I will only discuss fatty acids as our second ingredient and refer to them as fatty acids or oils for simplicity. Almost all natural soap makers use vegetable, fruit, or nut oils in their soap. You will find some that use animal fats but not that many. A good majority of our customers frown on the usage of animal fats. In almost all cases, you will use a combination of vegetable fruit oils or nut oils in your soap. Each oil contains a mixture of fatty acids, and each fatty acid imparts a different characteristic to your finished product. For now, as an example, coconut oil makes a very hard bar of soap and is very cleansing. The problem is, you should never use only coconut oil in your soap. There are very few fatty acids in coconut oil that moisturize or condition the skin resulting in a very drying bar of soap. Coconut oil alone will not produce a significant amount of creamy lather. No one will use a bar of soap that dries out the skin or does not lather very well. You have to combine your oils, so your bars provide a delicate balance of hardness, cleansing, lather, moisturizing, and conditioning. We will take a very close look at the different oils and the characteristics they impart to your soap in a subsequent chapter. We will also look at how to combine these oils for a perfect bar of soap and include recipes.

The third base ingredient necessary for your soap is liquid. You can use water, milk, beer, wine, juice, etc. The liquid you use will help determine what characteristics your final bar of soap will have. For example, goat's milk contains butterfat and the same lipids that are naturally produced by your skin. Goats milk will give your bars a higher level of moisturization than water. The liquid provides your soap with the characteristics it imparts and acts as the catalyst to begin the process of saponification. Depending on your production method, most water, or water in your liquid, will be cooked or cured out of your final product. We will also take a close look at liquids in a subsequent chapter.

You make natural bar soap by combining your lye with your liquid and letting it cool to a predetermined temperature between 100 and 130 degrees Fahrenheit. You heat your oils separately to this same predetermined temperature. Once your lye solution and your oils are at roughly the same temperature, they are mixed together, usually with a stick blender. All soap, independent of your final production method, starts in this way. At this point, the magic starts to happen. Your soap begins to saponify. As you blend your soap, it will start as a runny liquid. It will then begin to thicken up. This process of thickening up is called 'coming to trace.' Once your soap has reached trace, it is either ready to cook for hot process soap or liquid soap or ready to enter your moulds for cold process soap. In this chapter, we are talking about the process and science of making soap. Subsequent chapters will look at the above in detail and how to accomplish this with ingredients and recipes.

What is saponification? It is a chemical reaction between your alkali, fatty acids, and liquid. It is the actual process of creating soap. As your soap begins to thicken and saponify, you will notice that as you lift your stick blender out of the soap, it will start to leave ridges that take a couple of seconds to settle back down into the soap. This is called trace. There are three stages of trace, light, medium, and heavy. For light trace, a ridge will sink back into the soap quickly. A medium trace will take a little longer to sink back in. Heavy trace will not sink back into your soap. The ridge of soap will stay on top of your batch. Once a batch of soap has reached a light trace, it has started the process of saponification. For hot process soap, you will want to achieve a heavy trace. You will want to achieve light or medium trace for cold process soap to add additives and get them mixed in easily. During the cooking or curing process, your soap will complete the process of saponification.

All carrier oils, olive, coconut, castor, etc., are chemically composed of fatty acids and plant matter. They are known as triglycerides. Triglyceride broke down to its root word is tri, meaning three, and glyceride, representing glyceride. Carrier oils at a molecular level are considered three-chain fatty acid molecules. A carrier oil molecule is comprised of three molecules of fatty acid bound by one molecule of glycerin. To help visualize this concept, consider the capital letter E. As your soap goes through the chemical process of saponification, the fatty acid separates from the glycerin. The molecule is no longer bound. During this chemical process of saponification, the lye is consumed, the glycerin separates from the fatty acid, and the fatty acids are transformed into crystallized salts. The glycerin mixed back into the crystallized salts. There is no lye left in the final product.

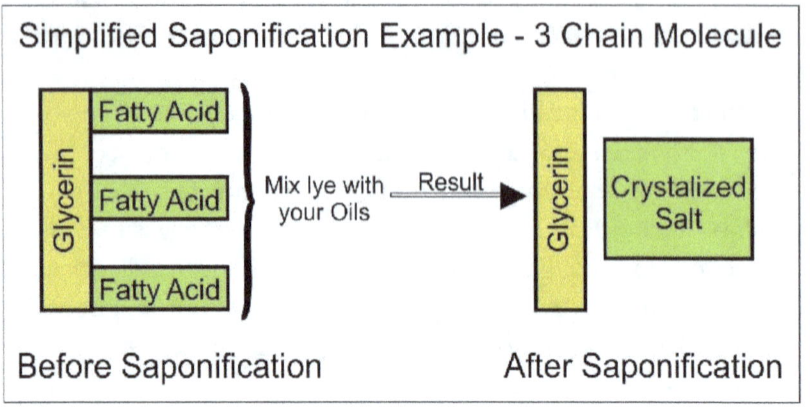

Completed natural soap is a combination of crystallized salts, water, glycerin, plant matter, and additives. That is one of the reasons you should not see the Word lye on an ingredient label. There is no lye left in the soap. For example, if you used lye, water, and olive oil to make natural soap, your ingredients list would not be lye water and olive oil. Your ingredients list would be 'aqua' representing water, glycerin, and 'sodium Olivate' representing your saponified olive oil or the crystalized salt of olive oil that remains. These are the International nomenclature of Cosmetic Ingredients (INCI) label listings. I will take an in-depth look at this in a subsequent chapter and also give you a comprehensive list of ingredients that includes the INCI term, botanical term, and common term for each of your possible ingredients when considering labelling. Each country will have its own requirements between these three choices. For example, in Canada, without exception, the INCI term must be used on the label. The botanical name for an ingredient is generally accepted in the US. If you were to use the common term, you would not list lye on the label. Remember, there is no lye left in the soap. You would use the term 'saponified olive oil.'

Okay, that completes an elementary 101 course on what natural soap actually is and how it is created. Although this section is a little technical, you will be much better prepared to answer your customer's questions when they ask if you make your soap with lye. You will get this question frequently. Most customers do not understand that you can only make natural soap with lye. Being armed with the knowledge of the science of soap and describing the process will set them at ease, not to mention how impressed they will be with your knowledge.

Soap Making Methods
Hot – Cold - Combined

*"Completing a task my way does not
make your way wrong. The outcome will
be differently the same."*
—Brian Cockell

NOW THAT WE UNDERSTAND A LITTLE BIT ABOUT the science of soap, it is time to look into the different production methods. Don't be concerned about the terms of some processes or equipment discussed in this chapter. We will be covering the actual making of soap, ingredients, additives, testing of soap, and so on in-depth in subsequent chapters. There are three main ways you can make soap. They are called hot process, cold process, and hot/cold process. I will address each one of these methods and give you both the pros and cons of each. Keep in mind through this discussion that different soapmakers will vehemently swear by one process or the other. You will read one book that tells you only to make cold process soap, another hot and another to use the combined hot and cold process method. Each method has its merits and its faults. Don't dismiss one method over the other without understanding what these merits and shortcomings are. You will need to determine what method, or methods, you will use to set up your soap studio with the required equipment. In our soap studio, we use both the hot and cold processes for different reasons, as you will see. So let's get into the discussion.

Hot Process Soap (HP)

When you make soap, you will generally mix your oils in a pot and heat them. You will then combine your lye with your liquid and let it cool a little. Then you will stick blend your oils and lye water and bring this mixture to trace. All soap begins this way independent of your final process to bring it to completion – saponification. You might include a couple of additives in this initial step, like clays, colourants, or silk, etc. After bringing your soap to trace, the hot process method entails cooking it to complete the saponification process.

Most soapmakers will mix their soap in a CrockPot and then cook it to complete the saponification process in the pot. Some will use a double boiler, but the CrockPot is oh so easy. Depending on the size and type of CrockPot you use, this cooking process will take one to two hours. Once your soap has finished cooking and cooled a little, you will now add your essential oils and, in some cases, your colourant or other additives if they are sensitive to lye. Don't forget, once the soap has fully saponified, there is no lye left if you have calculated your lye/oils ratio correctly, so it is now safe to add these lye-sensitive ingredients. You will then put your soap into your moulds to harden and cure.

The following day you will unmold the loaf or block and cut your soap into bars. Although technically, you could take a bar right up to the shower and use it, you will want to let it cure in a curing rack for a week or so. The reason for this is you will most likely be selling your bar by weight. As the soap bars cure, they will harden up and dissipate some of the water out of them. Your bars will lose up to 20% of their weight during this curing period from this water loss. After the curing process, your soap bars are ready to be wrapped and sold.

There are two main advantages to the hot process method. Firstly, the soap is technically ready to use once it hardens by the next day and prepared for sale in about one week. Having soap made quickly for the market is a significant advantage as you grow your business and have many soaps you need to keep in inventory. There is less worry about running out of inventory. If you check out some of the soapmaker websites, you will see that a good portion of their offering is not in stock more often than not. Having your soap always in stock is one way you can set yourself above your competition. You can also speed up the curing process with dehumidification if you need soap the next day.

The second significant advantage of hot process soap is you will not damage your essential oils or additives. You add your essential oils and lye-sensitive additives after your soap has saponified and cooled. Hot process soap cooks in the 180-190 degree Fahrenheit range. Essential oils lose their therapeutic value and scent when exposed to heat for a prolonged period. If you overheat your essential oils, you will damage their therapeutic properties and lose a good portion of their scent, defeating the purpose of adding them in the first place. Not all, but a good portion of your colourants and additives are also lye sensitive. When added directly to lye or unsaponified soap, they will turn your soap brown, or your additives will become ruined. With an equal amount of essential oil added to both hot process and cold process soap, your hot process soap will have a much stronger scent.

Although possible, it is difficult to achieve an intricate swirl design in your hot process soap as the batter is more like wet mashed potatoes when moulded.

Your hot process soap bars will have a more rustic look than your cold process bars. Some consider this rustic look to be inferior to a more polished look. I personally do not think so. I love a rustic-looking bar of soap, and it highlights natural and artisan-made. I strongly prefer the hot process method for its advantages, but the cold process does have its place. We will discuss that next.

Cold Process Soap (CP)

When you make cold process soap, as above, you mix all of your ingredients under heat together between 100 and 130 degrees and bring it to trace. In the cold process method, you bring it to light trace. Unlike hot process soap, you have to add all your other ingredients to the pot or bowl once your soap has reached trace, including your essential oils and other additives. Other than heating your oils and lye mixture, there is no cooking involved in cold process soap. You bypass the CrockPot or double boiler stage.

This complete mixture is now added to a mould and set aside to complete the curing and saponification process. During the initial curing phase, the mould's soap can reach temperatures up to 180 degrees Fahrenheit and remain at this temperature for quite some time. In two to three days, you will unmold this soap and cut it into bars. You will have to wear rubber or latex gloves for the cutting as the bars will still be chemically hot and not yet saponified. Once cut, the soap bars will be set aside for up to 6 weeks to complete the saponification process and neutralize the lye. After these six weeks, they will be ready for labelling and the market.

Some soapmakers will cover their moulds with towels or blankets for the first two or three days to maintain the high heat and ensure the initial saponification event includes the entirety of the bar. If the heat is not maintained, the soap can develop a discoloured ring in the middle of the bar if heat is not maintained uniformly through the initial curing stage.

Other soapmakers will put the cold process soap moulds directly into the fridge or freezer to slow down and reduce this natural heat generation. Doing this can also avoid a discoloured ring in the center of the bars. They do this to attempt to preserve some of the essential oil scents from being ruined by the heat. They will also do this to prevent milk soap from having its milk scald, turning the soap brown.

Cold process soap is superior to hot process soap for swirling. You mould cold process soap at light trace. The soap can be easily poured into the moulds at light trace and remains in a reasonably liquid state. Soapmakers will pour layers of different coloured soaps into a mould for a layered or swirled effect. They will also pour a primary colour overlayed by a secondary colour and then swirl the soap with a tool like a chopstick or a fork to create a pleasing design. Cold process soap is easier to swirl or layer than hot process soap.

It is also easier to place embeds in cold process soap. For this, you will want your soap at a medium trace or a little thicker. Embeds are objects or other soap shapes premade and embedded into your soap mould. Soap embeds generally differ in colour from your soap batter.

If you plan to make goat's milk or milk soap, the cold process method is the only viable method you can use without scalding your milk and turning your batch of soap brown. Some have tried and claim they make goat's milk soap with the hot process method. I have seen the videos. It's possible, but the process of turning your crockpot on and off, trying to maintain the heat below the scalding and discoloration temperature of the milk, is next to impossible and significantly increases your cooking time. I would never want to make 500 bars of soap under this condition. Milk is also very susceptible to heat damage. I recommend you use the cold process method for milk soaps. Cold process soap produces a smoother-looking, more dense bar of soap. Some prefer this feel and look.

One of the drawbacks of cold process soap is the curing time. Five to six weeks, at a minimum, is the generally accepted curing time. Of course, you will test your bars after they have cured to ensure they are no longer chemically hot – more on this later. It is not possible to drastically speed up this five to six-week period.

Another drawback to the cold process method is your essential oils and additives exposure to lye. Lye damages the scent and therapeutic characteristics of essential oils. Some additives are discoloured or ruined when exposed to lye, as mentioned above.

Hot process, cold process, Oven Process (HPOP)(CPOP)(HPCP)

You will read and hear about the hot and cold process hybrid method of making soap with many different acronyms. Different soapers give it different names. With this method, rather than mixing and cooking your soap in a CrockPot and then adding your essential oils and additives after it cools, you will combine all your ingredients in a bowl in the same way you do cold process soap. At this point, rather than moulding it and setting it aside to cure for six weeks, you will pour your soap into a heat-safe mould or soap pan and cook it in the oven at the lowest temperature of 170 degrees Fahrenheit. It will gently cook over time. You would generally put it in the oven before bed and remove it in the morning when you wake up.

Don't confuse this method with making hot process soap on a stovetop instead of a CrockPot. Some soapers will cook their soap in a pot on the stove rather than in a crockpot. I don't recommend these methods as you do not want to be using lye around areas you prepare food, so I do not teach them. Use a CrockPot for hot process soap. The only exception to this is if you have a dedicated oven, but I still prefer the crockpot method for cooking soap.

The only advantage of this method is having completed soap ready to use in the morning. Although this is a significant advantage, I don't believe it is worth sacrificing the value of your essential oils or additives with the heat. You have this same advantage with hot process soap made in a CrockPot without damaging your oils and additives. You can not produce milk soap with this method unless you want brown soap.

The other problem with this method is it is prone to having pools of glycerin throughout the soap. In Hot process, your glycerin pools on the top of the soap batch as it cooks and then gets mixed back into your soap. In the cold process method, glycerin does not separate into pools because of the long, gentle saponification process over time. In this hybrid method, the glycerin can, at times, pool in little glycerin pockets in your soap. Remember, the process of saponification separates glycerin from fatty acids. You will find many soapmakers that swear by this method. I am not one of them for the listed reasons.

Summary

After looking at these three methods and weighing the pros and cons, you will have to decide what method, or methods, you will use to make your soap. Although I prefer the hot process method for the reasons stated, I use the cold process method for goat's milk soaps and add extra essential oil to compensate for the loss of scent due to the lye exposure. I do not use the hybrid method. Each process has its merits. There are no rules. You will have to decide how you will make soap based on the information. I would also encourage you to look at other resources describing and teaching these methods to help you decide. It would be good to try each method to learn the ins and outs during your decision stage. There is no better teacher than hands-on. You might decide to use one, two or all three methods. There are no rules. It is a preference. Once you make your decision, you are ready to set up your equipment in your soap studio. We will look at this next.

HAVING A PLAN
Plan For Today, Be Ready for Tomorrow

"If you don't have time to do it right,
when will you have time to do it again?"
—John Wooden

PLAN FOR TODAY. BE READY FOR TOMORROW. What does this mean? It means that you should not be shortsighted when planning your workspace. Sure, you are going to be making small batches of soap to start. As your business begins to grow, and it will most likely grow quickly. You don't want to be making changes in your workspace every week, month, or quarter because of poor planning, moving raw materials from here to there to fit your expanding inventories.

Create your workspace for larger batches than you will initially be making, having enough space to produce, cure and cut your soap bars, etc. Poor planning is inefficient, wastes time, and costs money. Plan your workspace in size and function, assuming your business is going to grow and grow fast.

At this point, you should have an idea of what you will be making, how many bars you are planning to sell month by month, and what your growth strategy looks like through year one and beyond. You know this because you have completed your business plan. (Because you have already read this book through and are on your second reading as you execute your plan, right?) You will not be able to plan, to the soap bar, how many you will be selling in three months or your first year. However, if your business plan is solid and reasonable, you should be able to forecast somewhere close to what your sales will be. Plan your soap studio for what you plan to sell 12 months from now, not the first month.

When planning your workspace, you want to plan your production flow meticulously. Designing your production flow for continuous movement of your product from raw material to packaging in the most efficient way is paramount. When you finish one task, you want to move right into the next task efficiently. Simply stated, your goal is to take the least amount of physical steps from the start of production to your product's finishing. This might not sound like a big deal when starting in a small space, and it really isn't, but it will be as you grow. It helps you to develop good production habits on day one. Inefficient production flow is a massive time-waster, especially as your business begins to grow. Once you have employees, do you want them travelling all around the workspace, retrieving items from this corner or that corner and back again, or producing soap efficiently? That's a rhetorical question, chuckle. Of course, you want them to make soap most efficiently. Starting on your own, you also want to preserve your time by not wasting it in this same manner. As we discussed earlier, time is your greatest asset and your greatest enemy. Don't needlessly waste it.

The best way to plan your production flow is to consider all of the production process steps. Sequentially number each step from the start of the production process to the end of the production process. For example, step one will be to print or get the recipe for what you will make. Step two will be to gather your safety gear. Step three will gather the ingredients, step four to measure the ingredients into mixing bowls, step five to combine and heat your carrier oils, and so on. Once you have established the order of operations, you then design work stations within your production area in this order, allowing yourself to move from station to station, completing the process in the most efficient way possible.

The only exception to this production flow is when you have to consider safety. As an example, Lye needs to be segregated from your main work area to avoid raw lye contaminating or getting near any of your raw materials, work counters, pots, or utensils. In this case, you will create a lye mixing station away from your main production flow. This station will also need to be vented to the outside if you are mixing lye indoors. More on this later on. When it comes to safety, you will want to ensure you have your goggles or mask, latex or rubber gloves, and a long-sleeve smock readily available at or near stage one. You will also need to ensure you install your safety items at the appropriate stations. For example, you will want a proper fire extinguisher installed where you heat oils, an eyewash station installed where you mix lye, and white vinegar solution spritzer bottles handy where you are handling lye, or uncured soap. More on this later on as well.

You will most likely be making bar soap in one of two ways, either hot process or cold process. If you have chosen the hybrid method, this is fine as well. Below is a chart of activities you will need to consider when planning your production area for both hot and cold soap-making processes. Here is an example of a sample layout for a rectangular workspace. You will need to design your workspace in the most efficient way within your work area.

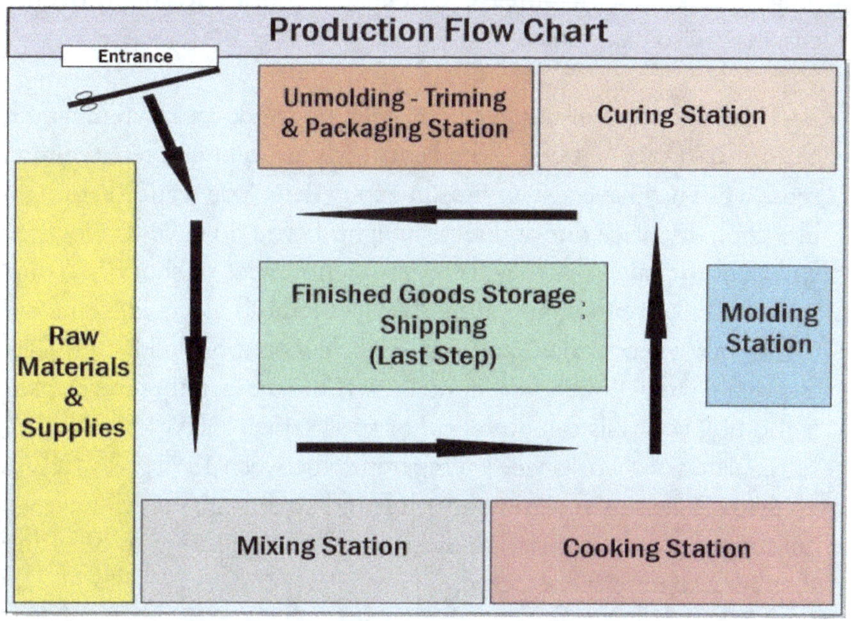

A well-planned production area will allow you to flow from station to station efficiently, completing each task, eliminating unnecessary steps, and completing your product production in the shortest amount of time. Proper planning will allow you to get to your next task quicker as you go through your production sequence. Spending time designing your production area in the beginning is essential. Don't skip this step, or you will find yourself continually moving things from here to there and back again as your operation grows. Avoid this frustration at the outset.

Two more items you will want to consider when planning your production area are lighting and power. You will want to ensure that you have plenty of light throughout your studio. Soapmaking involves reading digital thermometers, small scale measurements, and the physical inspection of different stages of work in progress. You will want to ensure that your light is adequate to accomplish these tasks.

Power is the other essential that you do not want to run short on. You will be running stick blenders, heating elements, crock pots, a microwave, and most likely have a fridge to preserve sensitive oils or an exhaust fan to vent lye fumes. You will need enough dedicated plugs to run multiple appliances at the same time. If you do not have enough power in your soap studio, have it installed. You don't want to be continually moving plugs around, resetting breakers, or changing fuses. Regularly overloading circuits is also dangerous.

The last couple of things to consider are windows and temperature. Your carrier oils, butters, and essential oils are light and temperature-sensitive. They have a shelf life, an expiry date. You want to store them in a cool, dry place out of direct sunlight. If you do have windows, you will want to make sure they have zero-light drapes or shutters. Your oils are also sensitive to temperature. If your studio is too cold, some of your carrier oils will crystalize, and others like coconut oil will be virtually impossible to get out of the container. If the temperature in your studio is too hot, your oils can go rancid or spoil rather quickly. You will want to regulate your workspace's temperature between 15 degrees Celsius and 18 degrees Celsius at all times, winter and summer. You will have a fair amount of money invested in these oils. You don't want to be losing them due to improper storage.

Designing your soap studio can be both challenging and fun. Keeping the above recommendations in mind during your design phase will help you be more efficient in production and save you valuable time overall. You will ultimately save money on wasted or spoiled raw materials and have a productive, pleasant, safe atmosphere in which to work. If you are already experimenting with soap production or are well on your way, there is no time like the present to make adjustments. It is better to take each of these considerations into account now rather than trying to adjust things monthly as you grow. You will thank yourself in the future for smart planning today.

SETTING UP SHOP
Equipment and Tools

"A big business starts small."
—*Richard Branson*

HOPEFULLY, BY THIS POINT, you have decided what type of business you will run, a proprietorship, a partnership, an LLC, or a corporation. You should have a dedicated space selected and set up for your soap studio. You should have a good idea of how you will produce your soap, hot process, cold process, or the hybrid method of hot and cold process. With these tasks completed or with the necessary decisions made, you are ready to set up your soap studio with tools and equipment. We are not discussing raw materials or ingredients for your soap. We will cover the actual making of soap in an upcoming section. Here we will discuss the tools, equipment, and accessories you will need for a functioning soap studio.

When it comes to setting up your soap studio with the required equipment, there are three ways you can go, budget, middle of the road, or the best, when it comes to equipment and supplies. With some items, you are not going to want to spare any expenses. With others, you can get away with going a little cheaper. We will discuss each option as we travel through this section.

One of my initial challenges in setting up my shop and getting started was finding the equipment and supplies I needed to do the job properly. In some circumstances, I chose inferior equipment that either broke soon after purchase or was not good enough to get the job done efficiently. One example is electronic handheld thermometers to test temperatures through the soapmaking process. I initially chose cheap plastic electronic thermometers from China sold by a soapmaking supplier that was not calibrated properly and stopped working soon after purchase. Sometimes the calibration was out by 20 degrees when tested against a mechanical thermometer. Inferior equipment won't do when making soap. It is a precise science. After four attempts, I eventually found a spectacular electronic metal handheld thermometer with perfect calibration that I am still using today. The moral of the story, going cheap in some circumstances will cost you more in the end.

To help you avoid some of the pitfalls of choosing the wrong or inferior equipment, wasting your time, and incurring extra expense. I have included a link at the end of this chapter that will take you to a listing of all the equipment, supplies, and accessories I use and where I purchase them. You can also find this link in the Appendix at the end of the book. This resource includes choices for budget, middle of the road, and expensive with my recommendation on what I believe to be the best items for the job based on my experience and testing. I also have it broken out by some countries so you can shop locally. I do not personally sell these items. The resource includes links you can click to make online purchases from the seller to have these items delivered to your soap studio. This will save you an incredible amount of time, frustration, and money. Alternately, of course, you can do your own research or find your own supply sources. The companion videos in the Appendix will also give you a visible view of the items I use. Below is a listing of what you will need.

Work Tables

One of the first items you will need is the work tables. Your work tables are where everything happens. I highly recommend stainless steel tables or, at a minimum, tables with a stainless steel top. Tables are one of those items where you will spend a little more, but it is highly worth it in the long run. You will be working with lye. You will be dripping lye solution and will have a micro-spray when mixing. As careful as you are, pots will inevitably boil over and mixing bowls spilled. You need to be able to quickly and effectively be able to clean your work surface. Stainless steel is resistant to lye and easy to clean. You will also be sterilizing your work surfaces and equipment frequently.

Stainless steel is the easiest surface to clean and disinfect. Stainless steel tables are also more rigid and have a better surface to use a scale on than the other choices. You want your scale on a flat, stable surface. Stainless steel is not heat-sensitive like the alternatives. You can work with hot  pots, heated oil, and hot lye solutions directly on the table. Stainless steel is also chemical resistant to any spills you might encounter. Here is an example of the tables I use in my soap studio.

The middle of the line choice is plastic tables. Although they are cheaper, much cheaper, and will work, they have many drawbacks. They are not as easy to clean as stainless steel and will pick up and be tainted with scents and discoloration over time. They can be sensitive to heat, are not very stable, and tend to sag as they get older. This sagging makes them unsuitable to use your scale on them as your scale needs an entirely flat surface to get an accurate reading. They can become pitted from chemical spills and are more difficult to sterilize, especially as they age. If you are going to use plastic tables, I recommend covering the surface with wax, parchment, or freezer paper. Your soap studio is essentially the same as a commercial kitchen. You never see plastic tables in a commercial kitchen. I do not recommend using them.

Your budget choice is wooden tables. Some new soapers will make this choice to save some money on startup. You can also make them yourself if you want. Wooden tables are a terrible choice. They will absorb everything spilled on them and maintain those scents. They are next to impossible to clean properly or sterilize. With wooden tables, you also risk contamination in your soaps from wooden particles as they degrade. Over time, wooden tables become damaged by lye and other chemicals you will use. Never use a wooden table unless you cover the surface with wax, freezer, or parchment paper. These papers are, of course, an additional expense every time you make a product. I highly recommend you do not use wooden tables.

Storage Cabinets

One of the next items you are going to need to consider is storage cabinets. You will need a place to keep all your soap supplies, packaging supplies, raw materials, and finished goods. You will be surprised as you go along and develop your business at how much storage you will actually need. Everything you collect or use for your business should have a place, and everything should be in its place. We considered this concept a little earlier.

There is nothing more frustrating than spending your valuable time looking for an item you need now. As you place cabinetry, drawers, and tool holders throughout your soap studio, locate these items in the proximity of where you are going to use them. For example, the location where we unmold, cut, and trim soap is located in a center island, the last stop in our production process, with drawers underneath the stainless steel work area to keep knives and trimers and other items we use for this process. We keep table holders for silicone spoons, spatulas, and whisks on our stainless steel tabletops next to our mixing and cooking areas. You want to consider ease of access and have your items nearby where you use them.

You will also want sturdy cabinets to house your items. Oils, butters, waxes, and additives are weighty. As your business grows, the size of containers will grow. We now deal with 50-pound bags and buckets of raw materials. Only a sturdy cabinet or storage location will be suitable for these items. Don't forget, plan for tomorrow, not just today.

The other consideration for your cabinetry is light. Carrier oils, butters, essential oils, and some of your additives are sunlight-sensitive, some more than others. If exposed to too much sunlight or heat, they will go rancid quickly. Store these items in a cool dark place. You do not want to be installing cabinets for these items with a bunch of windows in them. If you have cabinets with windows, cover the inside of the glass with a dark substance or paint. You also want to be storing your heat-sensitive items near the floor in your cabinets where it's cooler.

The best option is steel cabinets. They are sturdy and easy to clean. Steel cabinets come in many shapes and sizes and have adjustable shelving. We use steel cabinets and drawer units throughout our soap studio. They are my recommended cabinet.

Some soapers will use shelving units. Shelving units work fine as long as you do not have them exposed to direct sunlight. One trick with shelving units is to attach a dark sheet to the front face to help protect the inventory from direct light.

Wood or laminate cabinets are the second choice. The only real difference with wood is the shelves or drawers are harder to clean and should be lined with parchment paper or sealed with a wood sealer.

Wood can be as expensive as steel and sometimes more expensive unless you are building them yourself.

Your third choice is plastic. I would encourage you to steer clear of plastic shelving and drawers. In almost all circumstances, they are flimsy and not very stable. Unless you're prepared to spend a lot of money on quality plastic cabinets and drawer units, I recommend you avoid them.

Although not technically cabinets but rather storage units, you will want to consider a fridge and a freezer. You will have some carrier oils like grapeseed oil as an example that have a shorter shelf life. Grapeseed oil only has a shelf life of six months. Other raw material inventory items like vitamin E and rosemary olerin extract, to name a few, are very light and heat sensitive. You should store light and heat-sensitive ingredients in a refrigerator to extend their shelf life.

If you plan to make milk or goat's milk soap, you will need a freezer for two purposes. First, to store your goat milk and freeze it. Frozen Goats milk is mixed with lye to prevent scalding as the solution heats up from the lye. Two, for cooling your milk soap after you put it in the mould to prevent scalding of the milk. Some soapers will put all of their cold process soap into a fridge or freezer to prevent uneven heating and circle marks in the soap.

In our soap studio, we use a stand-up freezer to freeze our goat's milk. We raise Dwarf Nigerian Goats on our farm for their milk. These goats have the highest butterfat content of all the goat breeds at around 6.5%. This milk makes an exceptionally creamy, moisturizing bar of soap. Whether 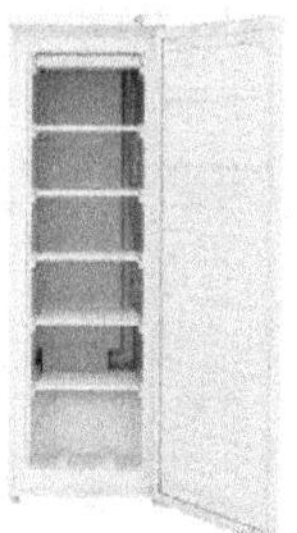 you raise goats for the milk or buy goat's milk from a supplier or use powdered goat's milk, you will need to freeze it if you do not want brown bars of soap. Stand-up freezers are hard to find. Take a look at the resource link at the bottom of this chapter to see some locations that sell them. We use a bar fridge with the face blacked out for our sensitive oils and additives. They are much smaller than regular refrigerators and work just fine. You could also use a standard fridge freezer combination.

When planning your setup, plan to have enough cabinets placed in convenient locations throughout your soap studio. If you do not have enough storage, you will very quickly find yourself working in a chaotic environment with stuff slammed all over the place and in every corner, nook, and cranny. An unorganized soap studio is not a pleasant, efficient, enjoyable environment with which to work. Plan your space and storage carefully.

Small Appliances

CrockPots

Now that you have some working tables and storage, your next step will be to outfit your soap studio with some required small appliances. You are going to have to heat oils, butters, waxes, and so on. If you are making hot process soap, you will need CrockPots. They are far superior to double boilers. I have tested almost every model and make out there and have always returned to the original CrockPot. They are simplistic, reliable, and cook evenly. I get 3 to 4 years of use out of one of these. When CrockPots are on sale, they are cheap. To cook soap, you do not need fancy ones. I can have up to 8 crockpots running during a soap cook.

You will want a Crockpot with three settings, warm, low, and high. I also prefer the crockpots that have lids that clamp down. The 7-quart pot is the preferred size. Our loaf moulds hold 16 bars of soap. The 7-quart is perfect for this mould size. No matter how many CrockPots you will use for a single cook, always have an extra one in inventory. The last thing you want to do is have a Crockpot break down in the middle of a cook. There is nothing worse than losing a whole batch of soap, have a backup.

You also will want all of your Crockpots to be the same size and the same make. Each size and different make of crockpot will cook at different temperatures. You want to keep things uniform for each batch. You do not want to be adjusting cooking times and temperatures as you cook. You also want to use the same type and size as you do not want to be trying to match what bowl goes in what pot after the cook and cleaning. You want all your ceramic crockpot bowls to be interchangeable, making life easier In the long run and saving you time. Below is a picture of my preferred Crockpot.

Convection Burners

You will need the means to heat your oils, butters, and some additives before blending with your lye solution for cold process soap. Different soapers will use different methods. Some will use a microwave. Although microwaves work, they are not my preferred method. With a microwave, you have to open the door to repeatedly stir, test temperatures, and then reset the microwave each time you perform one of these tasks. It is also too easy to overheat your solutions with a microwave. The biggest drawback is you are also limited in the size of batch you can heat at once. One positive to using a microwave is they are tabletop units and don't take up much space. Although they are not the best for heating your oils, they have their place, which we will look at in a bit. I do not recommend using microwaves to heat your oils.

Some soapers will use a full oven with burners, as found in most home kitchens. These units are fine but cumbersome and take up a lot of space. Ovens with burners also require a 220-volt outlet. Most soap studios will not have a 220-volt outlet available in their soap studio. They are overkill unless you are going to be using the hybrid method HPOP, as discussed earlier. With this method, you will need the stove to cook your soap overnight. I do not recommend HPOP or full oven-burner units.

The most versatile and recommended unit for heating your raw materials is what is called an induction cooktop. An induction cooktop is a small, flat tabletop unit that plugs into a standard 120-volt outlet. An induction cooktop uses a metal or induction pot. When you turn the heat on, it will only function if the pot is in place on the burner, so they are ultra-safe. The great thing about induction elements is that you can use

small to large pots and control the temperatures, just like a regular stove burner, to heat your oils slowly or quickly. They are also space-saving as they are small countertop units and lightweight. If you do have different heating areas in your soap studio, you can quickly move them around, have more than one, or put them away if you need the space when not in use. Induction elements are my preferred and recommended heating source. Below are pictures of the induction burners I use. I know these units will be new to some. You can find these units to buy by clicking or going to the resource link at the end of this chapter.

Microwaves

Ok, back to microwaves. Although not recommended to heat your oils, butters, and additives, they do have their place in a production environment. You will run into circumstances where you need to top up

an item's heat or have a minimal quantity to heat. When you are developing and experimenting with new recipes, you will also run into circumstances where you will want to add a pinch of heated this or that. Microwaves are quick and convenient for this purpose. If you trim your soap or if you make your soap in loaf moulds, most soapers do, you will have cut-off and trimmed soap pieces. You will need to rebatch these soap pieces into bars. Microwaves are the perfect tool to rebatch soap. I will teach you all about that in the soapmaking chapter. I recommend you have a small microwave on hand. It is best to have one that is 1200 WATTS or less. The more powerful ovens heat or reheat too quickly and take a lot of power.

Immersion Blenders

Before the advent of immersion blenders, soapers would add their lye solution to their oils and then manually stir the mixture to reach trace with a spoon or whisk. This manual process could take up to an hour. Ouch! Once immersion blenders, also known as stick blenders, hit the market, soapers figured out pretty quickly they could use this small appliance to bring their soap to trace in about 5 to 10 minutes. Thank goodness for the immersion blender. You can not live without this item. It is one of the best tools we use to speed up time and save our arms.

Like CrockPots, I have tested almost every immersion blender out there. There are a couple of things you want to watch for when choosing yours. These appliances come in very cheap models, from $10 to $20 to costly models over $300. You want to avoid the cheap ones. This is a tool you will use every time you make soap. The cheap ones do not have enough power to mix soap to thick trace and frequently burn out and break. You will be continually replacing them, costing yourself more money in the long run. The expensive ones are overkill and not necessary. A good middle-of-the-road model works just fine. You want to have one that is between 200 and 250 watts.

The next thing for consideration is its construction materials. Because you are mixing lye, you need to use one with a stainless steel shaft. The last thing you want in your immersion blender is a one-piece unit. The motor should detach from the shaft. You want to choose a two-piece unit for a couple of reasons. Firstly, as you blend your soap to trace, your blender will begin to heat up. You will want to switch it out if it gets hot with a new one to avoid burning out your motor. With having more than one on hand, you simply switch the tops, or motor section, leaving the mixing arm in the soap.

Secondly, it is much easier to clean a mixing arm that detaches from the motor base. My biggest complaint with the two-piece units is how well they do or do not come apart. Some of them twist together and snap into place. Avoid these. More often than not, they will come apart during your mixing as your mixture thickens and, after a while, won't stay together at all. The best ones are the ones that click together and have a manual button to separate them again. I have never had an issue with this type.

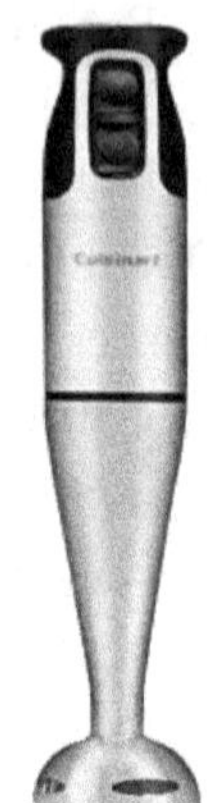

The last consideration with your immersion blender is how the mixing head looks. I have found the ones with a flat bottom create a suction on the pot's bottom, not allowing you to freely and smoothly blend. They suck themselves to the bottom of the pot. You want to choose a blender with a mixing head with ridges on its bottom to avoid this suction the flat ones can create. Below is a picture of the type I use and prefer after years of trial and error.

Grinders & Dehydrators

Although not necessary, you will find it convenient to have a small grinder and a small dehydrator on hand. You will run into circumstances where you want to reduce the size of a botanical, exfoliant, salt, or additive you are either adding to your soap or placing on top of your soap. A small adjustable coffee bean grinder works great for this application and is very convenient. One of the exfoliants we use in our exfoliating soap is eggshells. We dehydrate, then grind our eggshells with our coffee bean grinder to just the right consistency.

A small tabletop dehydrated will also come in handy. You can use this appliance to dehydrate botanicals and spices, whether you gather or purchase these items. They are also great to use if you have an order to get out the next day, and you need to speed up the cure time of your hot process soap.

Small Tools

Once you finish setting your soap studio up with your small appliances, it is time to gather your small tools and accessories. As with your other choices, you will have to decide on the quality of the items.

Scales

You are going to need two types of scales. All soap recipes need to be created and measured by weight, not volume. Never deviate from this practice. Each of your oils and butters will have a saponification value. Your saponification value is how many grams or ounces of lye you will need to saponify one gram or ounce of oil. If you are not exact with this measurement, you could end up with a bar of soap with unsaponified lye in it, known as hot soap. (Don't fret about this term or how it is derived. You will use a saponification app or website to calculate these values. I cover this in the soapmaking chapter). Soapers call this lye-heavy soap. You would have to discard this soap safely. We will discuss these values in-depth in a subsequent chapter. Your measurements need to be exact to avoid this error. You will need a micro-scale for small measurements. Your micro-scale should be able to measure one-tenth of a gram, or .0035 of an ounce and up, for your lye and additives. These small scales will have a weight limit and are not suitable for measuring your oils, butters, and liquids. You will need a second scale that can weigh items up to 5 kilograms or 11 pounds for these items.

You will measure many ingredients as you prepare your batch of soap. Some of these ingredients will be butters that are solid at room temperature. You will inevitably spill heated oils and butters on your larger scale. It happens to us all. When this happens, the oils or butters will leak into the scale buttons. You will eventually ruin your scale. For this reason, always choose a scale with sealed buttons on it that you can wipe off easily. You will save yourself from having to replace your scales frequently. A sealed unit is not as crucial for your smaller scale but also worth consideration. You are generally working with smaller amounts of material that are easier to weigh with your small scale.

For the same reason as above, I prefer using scales with a glass top for the larger scale. You can see through the scale and know if a cleaning below the scale top is required. Leaving gunk under the scale's top surface can throw off the weight, something we never want.

You want to avoid scales that shut themselves off after a short period. I literally ended up throwing a couple of my original scales out after learning this lesson the hard way. It is very frustrating to be a couple of ounces away from completing your measurement, only for the scale to turn itself off.

You can use mechanical scales as they are great for accuracy, although you will find them cumbersome over time. You will spend a lot of time with scales. Efficiency and ease of use are critical with scales. Electronic scales with a good backlight and a large display are optimal.

You will want to go at least the middle of the line when it comes to your scale choice. The top of the line is better. Scales are one of those areas where you do not want to scrimp. Inferior scales will not be accurate and will not last. I have done a lot of testing with scales. Below are the pictures of my preferred and recommended scales.

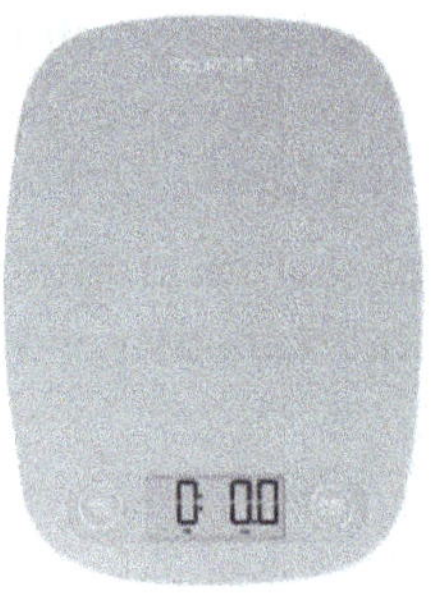 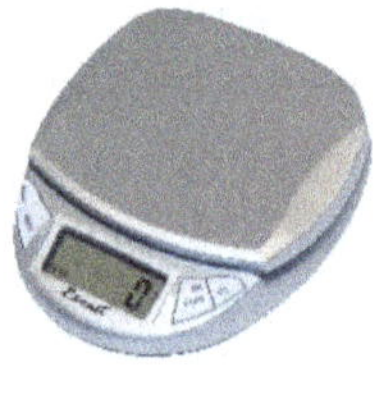

Thermometers

Next on the list of required tools are thermometers. Thermometers are items where you definitely do not want to go cheap. Getting your temperatures correct is paramount when making soap. If your temperatures are too low for cold process soap, your lye will not completely saponify. If they are too high for hot process soap, you will experience what we call a volcano with your soap batter while cooking. Volcanoing is a term we use in making soap where your batter volcanoes up and over the edge of your cooking pot. You also do not want to add heat-sensitive materials like essential oils to a pot of soap that is too hot.

You will burn the oils off or damage their therapeutic value. Temperatures are important. You want to get them right. I cover much more about temperatures in the soapmaking chapter.

You will want to choose thermometers with a minimum accuracy of +/- 2% of your reading with a measurement range from at least 0 degrees to 130 degrees Celcius or 32 degrees to 250 degrees Fahrenheit. You have three main choices when it comes to thermometers. What type you choose really boils down to preference and budget. Below are your main options.

Gun Thermometers

Your best and most expensive are what they call infrared gun thermometers. These thermometers can be pointed at your subject from 10" to 12" away, giving you a good accuracy reading. Like their name, they have a handle that resembles a gun. The displays are generally large and easy to read. They are also the most versatile. Most manufacturers calibrate these thermometers during final production.

A hybrid of the infrared gun thermometer is a handheld probe thermometer. This type also has a handheld base with a large display. A probe with a wire is attached to the base that you insert into your soap or oils. You will want to ensure the probe is stainless steel.

Both of these types of thermometers are rather large and very expensive. However, you will find many soapers that do use and swear by them. Because of their high cost and bulkiness, I do not use this type. You will most likely have different stations in your soap studio that require temperature readings. You will either have to move this item around with you or have more than one on hand if you don't want to be continually chasing down a single thermometer.

Pocket Thermometers

Your middle-of-the-line thermometer is called a pocket thermometer. As the name implies, you can fit them in your pocket. They are also available in two types, point and probe. The point type is similar to the above, with three differences. You need to hold them no more than an inch away from the item, they have a smaller display, and of course, they are smaller. Pocket thermometers also come pre-calibrated from the manufacturer. This is my preferred type for a couple of reasons. They are relatively inexpensive and accurate. Rather than moving a bulky, expensive thermometer around your soap studio, you can have two or three of these in your different locations where you take temperatures. The probe type is also small, with the probe directly attached to the head of the thermometer. You will want to make sure the probe is stainless steel. They are less expensive than the point type, and you can also have a number of them on hand. These are my wife's preferred type.

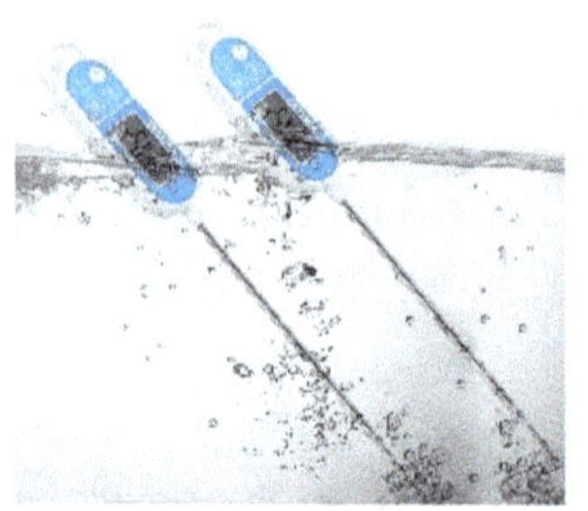

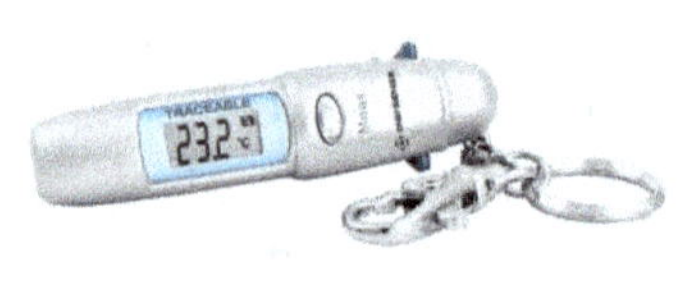

Mechanical/Mercury Thermometers

Your budget thermometer is the old mercury mechanical thermometer. If you do choose this type, ensure that the measuring tip is stainless steel. You never want a glass tip or aluminum tip in your lye. Aluminum has a very nasty reaction to lye, and you don't want to be breaking a glass-tipped thermometer in your soap batch. There is nothing wrong with using a mechanical thermometer. Although they are accurate, easy to use, and extremely cheap, I do not use them. I don't have the patience to be waiting for them to measure the temperature, and remember, your time is valuable. You don't want to waste it unnecessarily.

Measuring Cups, Mixing bowls, and Pots

You will need an abundance of measuring cups and mixing bowls. You have three main choices, glass, stainless steel, or plastic. The size of the batch you are making will generally dictate what measuring cup or bowl you use. When measuring your liquids, oils, butters, and additives, it is an excellent practice to measure all ingredients before combining and mixing. You want to do this for a couple of reasons. Firstly, you want to ensure you have enough of each raw material in stock before mixing them. If you get three-quarters of the way through a mix and then realize you are short of an ingredient, you will be in trouble. Given the sensitivity of getting everything correct for saponifying your lye, you cant substitute along the way. Secondly, you will be adding ingredients at different phases of production. You do not want to be leaving temperature-sensitive mixtures to cool or heat outside of their tolerance while you take time to collect and measure the next ingredient.

Measuring cups

I strongly prefer heat-resistant glass measuring cups for several reasons. They are the most versatile. These measuring cups have handles, so they are easy to move around and pour. They are also great for getting all of your ingredients into your pot using a spatula as you hold them by the handle. They come in a good selection of sizes. I use 1, 2, 4, and 8 cup capacity pyrex cups and use them for all of my hot process soap mixtures. You can also use them as double boilers by setting them in a heated pan of water with your ingredients. They are safe to use in

microwaves. You will hear from some soapers that these glass measuring cups will develop hairline cracks over time when exposed to lye. I am not sure of the validity of this claim. I am still using the same measuring cups I started with six years ago. They look to be in as good a shape today as the day I bought them with close inspection. I am not suggesting these claims are false. I am simply stating I have never experienced any issue with heavy use over time and therefore have no concern.

Your second main option for your measuring cups is plastic. You will find many soapers using plastic measuring cups. One of the main reasons is you can purchase them with funnel spouts that make pouring ingredients and soap for swirling easier. They also weigh less. You can certainly use plastic with no issue, and they are much less expensive.

I do not personally use them for a couple of reasons. Firstly, at higher temperatures, they are heat-sensitive. Secondly, they pick up odours and are hard to clean once they become damaged from use and scratches that occur over time. In some circumstances, you will want to see through your measuring cup. You are unable to see through the majority of plastic ones.

Mixing Bowls

Your best choice is stainless steel bowls. I use stainless steel bowls for cold process soap batches. (There are no bowls required for hot process soap as everything is mixed directly in your crockpot). Because I freeze my goat's milk, they are easier to use than plastic bowls. Once I add my lye water to the milk, I will gently heat the bowl's bottom on my convection stove to start the melting process at the bottom of the pot. I could not do this with plastic. One side effect of mixing

lye in stainless steel bowls is they will become dull over time. This dulling does not affect the quality or functionality of the bowls whatsoever. You can get these bowls in sizes from small to very large. They are a good choice. You can also use these bowls as double boilers in a pan of heating water. One drawback to stainless steel bowls is you cannot use them in the microwave. To heat oils for cold process soap, your best choice is stainless steel pots. I use stainless steel soup cauldrons for my cold process goat's milk soap. They also work with induction burners, as discussed above. Never use aluminum pots. Lye has an adverse reaction with aluminum making them very dangerous.

Your budget choice is plastic bowls. I never use plastic. I don't even own any plastic cups or bowls. Plastic has many drawbacks. As with measuring cups, they become damaged over time, discolour over time, and are not easy to clean once they become scratched and pitted. You cannot use them on your burner, and only some plastics are microwave safe. I do not use them because they pick up scents that are impossible to get out of the bowl. If you can tolerate the above issues or are on a strict budget, plastic will work, but I don't recommend them.

Pots

You will use pots for cold process soap to heat your oils and butters. You will heat your oils and butters in a pot in most cases. The only exception is if you are heating in a microwave. Not recommended as indicated above, but in this case, you will use a microwave-safe bowl.

Some will use a double boiler to heat their oils and butters. I find this to be tedious and unnecessary and takes way too long. Remember, time is money.

I use large soup pots to heat my cold process soap oils and butters. These give me the flexibility to cook either large or small batches. I will generally run two soup pots on my convection stoves for each cook's batch size of 150 bars. With this system, I can produce over 600 bars of soap a day. You can quickly scale this system up to meet growing demand.

Utensils

Silicone Spatulas and Spoons

Once you have all your fancy measuring cups, bowls, and pots, you are going to need some utensils. Here you have four main choices: silicone, stainless steel, plastic, and wood. When it comes to spoons and spatulas, I highly recommend you use silicone and stainless steel. Silicone stands up very well to lye, is extremely flexible to get every last drop out of your measuring cups and bowls, and is heat resistant. They come in small, medium,

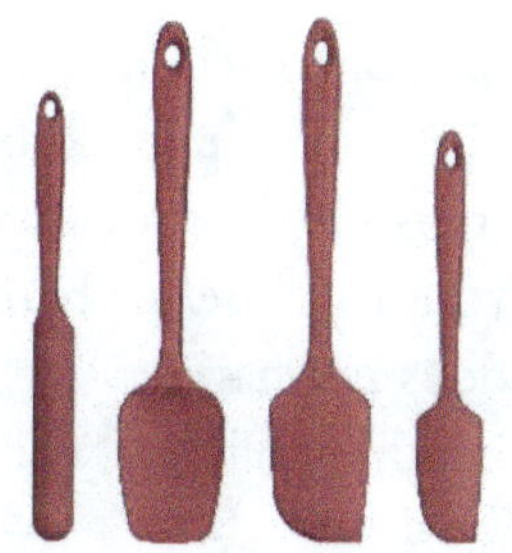

and large sizes. Silicon is also easy to handle as they are also slip-resistant in your hands. You will love using these. I have never found a drawback to using silicone utensils.

Stainless Steel Spoons

Stainless steel spoons are too ridged to get the contents out of cups, bowls, and pots. Use silicone. However, they are spectacular for digging solid raw materials like coconut oil or mango butter out of their containers. You should have at least one or two long-handled ones on hand for this purpose. It is best to choose ones with rounded handles on the top. You will spend a lot of time digging 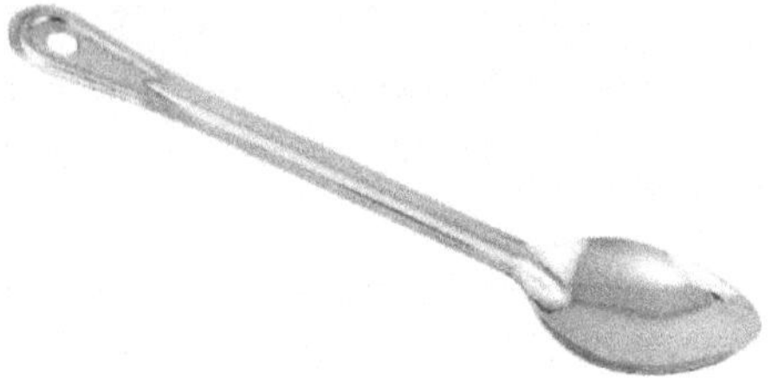 out hard oils. Steel spoons with handle tops that are square will hurt your hands over time. It would help if you had a couple of small stainless steel spoons on hand to manage small portions of lye and additives.

On the other hand, although plastic or wood is your budget choice, they are not preferred. Plastic utensils are rigid, and it is hard to get all your ingredients out of your cups and bowls. Like the plastic bowls, they pick up scents over time. I do not recommend them. Plastic spoons are prone to breaking when digging out hard oils and butters. Although some soapers use wood, you never should. Wood degrades over time with the use of lye and begins to splinter and deteriorate, leaving wood slivers in your soap batter. They also pick up scents and are impossible to clean. Avoid wooden spoons and spatulas at all costs.

Whisks

Your best choice for whisks is stainless steel with either silicone or rubber handles. Although you can get all stainless steel whisks, you will find that when you use them, the handles pick up lye condensation as the solution heats up when mixing. You don't want to  transfer this condensation that will get on your gloves elsewhere. This condensation does not happen with rubber or silicone handles. Silicone whisks are more challenging to clean than stainless steel.

The recommendation is stainless steel whisks with rubber or silicone handles.

Mortar & Pestle

Although not a requirement for your setup, Mortar and pestles come in handy for grinding small quantities of herbs and spices that you might add to your soap batter or sprinkle on top of a soap batch. These come in an unlimited variety of materials. You can purchase them in stone, wood, steel, plastic, and composite materials. I would choose a mortar and pestle based on all the recommendations listed throughout this section on utensils. I prefer and recommend a solid granite set for the weight and quality of this stone material. Plus, they look cool. Although I have a nice mortar and pestle set, I have never used it. I prefer to do my grinding in a coffee bean grinder, as mentioned above.

Funnels and measuring spoons.

Funnels will come in very handy. It is a good idea to have some small, medium and large funnels in your stock. You will find many uses for them. Like all the other recommendations, I recommend a good set of stainless steel funnels with long necks. Long neck funnels can sit by themselves in small neck bottles freeing your hands up for pouring and steadying the vessel you are filling. They do not pick up scents or become discoloured.

A good set of stainless steel measuring spoons is also a must. It would be best to have these spoon sets in both metric and imperial to avoid doing continual conversions when cooking. Sometimes you might be following a recipe in metric, other times in the imperial measurement system.

In addition to your large measuring cups, you will want to have a set of small stainless steel measuring cups on hand. You can purchase kits that come in sizes from $1/8^{th}$ of a cup to 1 cup. These kits are ideal.

I avoid plastic for all the reasons above that I do not use plastic for both of these items.

Storing Your Curing Soap

Once you begin making your soap, you will need somewhere to store your finished product as it cures before you put it in a retail package or bag. You will be designing and creating many different types of soaps, and you will be offering many different scents. Your natural soap will need to cure in racks with good airflow around the bars. Hot process soap will generally cure for about one week. Cold process soap will cure for about six weeks. Some soaps like pure traditional castile soap made with only olive oil can take 5 or 6 months to cure fully.

When you first start making soap, any stainless steel rack or plastic tray with slots will work. You will quickly find out that you are making more soap than you can store this way. You will shortly run out of places to place these curing racks. If you are making cold process soap, you will also need to keep cold process soap away from children and pets as the soap is still chemically hot until it fully cures (saponifies).

Investing in a good set of stackable curing racks is highly recommended. There are some great racks on the market, and some even designed explicitly for soap curing. You want your racks to be stackable, the correct size for your soap bars, and sturdy. It helps if you choose a set of racks that come on wheels to move them around. Don't forget that you will have to move them to your packaging area to be packaged and prepared to sell once they cure. I have seen some soapers use shelving.

Shelving is not ideal as you cannot move it around; it is hard to get to the higher shelves' back and challenging to rotate bars.

You will want to keep your curing racks out of direct sunlight and in a cool dark place with some airflow. Sunlight will damage the essential oils and some additives in your soap. Some oils are light-sensitive, especially oils with a short shelf life, and you do not want sunlight turning your soap rancid. You will also want to rotate your bars every two to three days to cure them evenly and speed up the curing process. Rotating bars is very easy when you have stackable racks.

Storing your Finished soap

The last item you will need to set up your shop and get ready for production is a place to store your packaged soap that is ready to be sold. Your soap will have an expiry date and shelf life. You will want to have a storage location that makes it easy to rotate your stock, meaning new soap goes to the back, and older soap is kept in the front to sell first.

Some soapers use shelving with roll-out shelves. Others use stackable plastic bins. You will find some soapers using a second or third set of curing racks. Your choices here are endless and up to your preference.

You should follow the same rules as curing. Have your stored soap inventory in a location out of the sun. A cool dark location is best. I use plastic stackable storage bins with drawers. I find they help keep the scent in my soaps as they are closed bins, and the bins take on the scent of the stored soap, helping to maintain that scent.

MOLDS AND CUTTERS
Getting your soap to the packaging Phase

*"The best investment is in the tools of
one's own trade."*
— Benjamin Franklin

BEFORE YOU EMBARK ON YOUR SOAP JOURNEY, you will need a couple of moulds and cutters. Due to the complexity of this topic, I have dedicated a chapter to it. It would be best to spend some time planning what your soap will look like before deciding what moulds and cutters to use. You will see many different styles of soap packaging and presentation on the market. Some soapers will create their soap in loaf or cylinder moulds and then cut these moulds into bars. These moulds usually produce 12 to 24 bars of soap. Some loaf moulds will accommodate up to 48 or 96 bars of soap. Once the bars are cut to size, some soapers will leave them as is with a rough top. Others will cut the rough top off to mimic a more conventional bar of soap. Some soapers will trim the edges of the bars to give a smoother feeling when first used. You can use loaf and cylinder moulds for both the hot and cold process soap-making methods. Using loaf or cylinder moulds is the most popular and productive way to make artisan natural soap but not the only way.

If you want to become a serious soaper, you have a singular goal. You want your soap to be functional for people to fall in love with it to the point they want to use it every day. You want them to replace their conventional store-bought synthetic detergent with your all-natural artisan soap. It has been my experience that the more professional your soap and packaging looks, the closer you come to achieving this goal. I cut and trim my soap to look like conventional soap while maintaining a natural look and feel to the packaging. I sell the soap as a daily use bar, not as decoration or just a gifting soap. People tend to look at fancy soap with high ridges on the top, sprinkles of this, or that on the bar, wrapped in only a paper sleeve as a gifting soap, and not something they will use for themselves every day.

If your goal is to sell one-off novelty bars of soap that people give as gifts, this is fine, but you will struggle to move your soap business from the novelty stage to the functional stage. If your goal is to establish a six-figure soap-making business, consider presentation and how to turn your customers into loyal, repeat customers. Customers using your soap daily, telling their friends about it, and giving you 5-star reviews are required, and presentation is vital. Customers need to see your soap as the only soap they will ever use. To accomplish this, they have to use it, not gift it. Once they use it and fall in love with it, they will then gift it as well—the best of both worlds. Present your soap as a natural artisan, professional daily-use soap and not just a novelty gift.

Soapers also use single bar silicone or plastic moulds. With these moulds, you fill one mould at a time with your soap batter. A mould usually contains 6 to 24 bars within the mould. Once the filled mould has gone through its curing time, each bar is removed individually. The single mould method is ok to use with the cold process soap-making method. You can use the hot process method, but it is challenging to get good-quality soap bars. Although not the most productive way to make soap, you can achieve some very intricately designed soap with this method. When you see fancy bars of soap like seashells, animals or angels, etc., silicone moulds have been used to mirror these shapes. There is value in having both daily use bars and fancy gifting bars as part of your product offering—a lot of customers like these fancy-shaped bars for guest bathrooms and to give as gifts.

When just starting, you will go through a testing phase as you experiment with recipes and the testing of your new soaps. For these test batches, you want to keep them small, as in one or two bars at most. You will most likely go through many phases of testing. There is no point in using a 12 or 16 bar mould for these tests unless you are making a proven recipe that you know will end up in bars for sale. Most new soapers do not want to spend money or time making test moulds.

The good news is, you can use several items found around your home for testing small batches. I have seen soapers use cleaned-out milk cartons cut to size, muffin tins with inserts, empty, clean margarine containers, the cut-out bottoms of plastic water bottles, and the list goes on. Be creative. You can use any container you find as long as it has been cleaned and is not made of aluminum. If you use anything from your kitchen, ensure you no longer use it for food preparation. If you are using items made of plastic, wood, or a material that is not flexible, you will need to line that material with a freezer or parchment paper to get the soap out of the chosen mould.

Once you are satisfied with your new soap, you will send it out to family and friends for customer testing. It is a good idea to send your test soap with a survey so your testers can report back to you on their experience. Then, if required, you will make more recipe adjustments and repeat the process until you are happy with your surveys and new soap. At this point, you can then increase your recipe size to the size of soap batches you will make during your production runs. Now you are ready to purchase or make your production moulds.

Loaf Molds

As indicated, loaf moulds are the most popular mould in use and the most challenging issue to wrap your head around. One option is to buy your moulds from soap supply companies or dedicated mould companies. You can purchase moulds in wood, plastic, composite materials, or silicone. If you use anything other than silicone, it is a good idea to line your moulds with a freezer or parchment paper before pouring your soap batter into the mould. By lining the mould, you will eliminate the hassle of removing your finished soap. A lot of soapers struggle in this area.

Breakaway moulds are the best as you can remove one side of the mould to get your soap out. Silicone moulds are excellent, but because they are not very rigid, you should place them inside a wooden outer mould to keep your soap bars' shape. Silicone moulds are excellent when it comes to releasing your soap from the mould due to their flexibility, and you do not need to line them with freezer of parchment paper, but you will have to wash them after each batch. My preference is a breakaway composite mould. If appropriately lined, you do not need to clean them after each use.

A standard bar of soap is 2" high by 3" long by 1" wide. A mould that is 2.5" high by 3" wide by 12.25" long will make 12 bars of 1" soap. The extra .5 of an inch on the height is to allow for a little extra soap batter in the mould to give you either ridges or an additional allowance to trim off as the top will not be smooth like the bottom and sides. The extra .25 of an inch on the length of the mould is to allow room to shave off the end cuts, so your two end cut bars are smooth and presentable. A trimmed bar of this size has an approximate cured weight of 125g. If you wanted to make 16 bars per batch, you would increase the mould's length by 4" to 16.25" and so on. If you're going to make a different sized bar, you would follow the above model for your bar size and do the calculations.

If you would like to make your moulds rather than purchase them, several mould blueprints are available on the internet. Simply search "Soap Mould Blueprints." You can see the moulds I made and use if you watch the soapmaking companion video to the book that is listed in the Appendix.

There are specific mathematical calculations to determine the batch's size to fill your mould or the size of the mould you will need for the batch size you have made. For anybody who is not a math expert, this becomes complicated. For a mathematical calculation, you have to calculate how much weight in grams fits into what size of a container measured in cubic inches. Remember, your soap ingredients are always measured by weight.

If you are not a math person or don't want to become involved in complex mathematical calculations to determine your mould size for each batch size, I have created a simple formula to follow. Once you mix your raw materials, you will either cook the batter for hot process soap and then go through a short cure time or cure the batter for about six weeks for cold process soap. Each 3 inch by 2 inch by 1 inch bar of soap weighs approximately 125g after curing. During the cooking and curing process, independent of the method you use, your soap batch will lose about 25% of its total water weight. Using this simple rule, you can now calculate how big a batch should be for your mould size or how big of mould for your batch size. It doesn't sound straightforward, but it is.

To look at an example. If you want to make a mould to hold 18 bars of soap and those bars will be the standard size of 2 x 3 x 1 inches. Your simple math would look like this:

(18x125)x1.25=2812.5 Your total batch weight will need to be 2825.5 Grams for an 18 bar soap mould of standard size bars.

The 18 represents the number of bars in the mould, the 125 represents the weight per cured bar, and the 1.25 means multiplying the 18 bar finished cure weight by 1.25%. This 25% represents the extra water in your batch that will cure out of the soap.

To calculate the weight of a different bar size to use in your formula, each cubic inch of soap weighs approximately 20.8g, so a bar size of 2 x 4 x 1 is eight cubic inches weighing about 166.4g. You would substitute 166.4 for the weight in your formula.

(18x166.4)x1.25=3744 Your total batch weight will need to be 3744 Grams for an 18 bar soap mould.

If you really hate math, and a lot of people do, there is another way to figure out how many grams your soap batch should be to fit a particular mould you might have. This method is not perfect but will get you close. Once close, some minor adjustments to batch size will get you to perfect. The water method is also an excellent method if you have a non-standard mould that is not uniform in shape.

For a loaf mould, line the mould with a leak-proof plastic bag. Fill the bag with water up to the height you will pour your soap into the mould. Then remove the bag and weigh it. Voila, this is roughly how much your soap batch should weigh to fit the mould. This method is not perfect but will get you very, very close. After making, curing and cutting your first batch, you can then make minor adjustments to your batch size to get it just right.

For a cavity mould, say a mould with 12 cavities, line one cavity with a leak-proof bag. A sandwich or small freezer bag works well. Fill the bag in the one cavity with water. Then take the bag out and weigh it. In our case, we want to use a 12 cavity mould, so simply multiply this weight by 12, and that will give you the rough size your soap batch should be. Once again, not a perfect method, but it will get you close. As in the loaf example, you can make small adjustments to your batch size to get it right.

There are many methods to calculate batch size for your mould. They range from complex mathematical equations to guestimations. I have presented a couple of the more straightforward ways here. The ones I follow. You can find many formulas to calculate volume on the internet if you are looking for a precise mathematical formula. I have excluded them here due to the complexity of these calculations that are not really necessary to arrive at a batch size for your mould size.

Cavity Molds

The above section touches mainly on loaf moulds. You also have the option to purchase a single bar or multiple bar cavity moulds. These moulds come in configurations from a single cavity mould to multi-cavity moulds from 6 to 24 cavities. Although you can find these  moulds made in many different materials, I strongly recommend using silicone moulds if you plan to go this route. With any other material, you will continuously struggle to get the soap out of the moulds. More often than not, you will damage your bars, trying to free them from the moulds unless they are silicone. Use these moulds with the cold process method. You will find them very difficult to fill with the hot process method.

Cutters

If you are producing your soap in either loaf moulds or cylinder moulds, you are going to need a way to cut these loaves or cylinders into bars. When soapers are just starting their business, they tend to do this by hand. By hand, I mean using a small tool to cut the soap into bars. I have seen some very creative tools and methods used to accomplish this. Be aware, with this hand-cutting method, your soap will look very 'Hand Made' unless you have a very steady hand and excellent hand-eye coordination. If you are selling your soap as an artisan's hand-made soap, this can be an advantage, but I believe your soap also needs to have a professional look and feel even if you are marketing your soap as handmade.

Examples of cutters you can use are drywall mud applicators, putty knives, plaster paste applicators for a ridged look, bread or butcher knives. I have even seen some soapers use hack saws, but that did make me chuckle. Use whatever works for you. One trick is to buy a mitre box from your local hardware store and cut your loaf using this box by running your cutting tool down and through the 90-degree cut line. Using these mitre boxes gives you a very smooth and even bar of soap. You can also build your own guide to control your cuts. Hand cutting your soap is the budget method, and you will probably quickly grow tired of the process and time it takes. This method is adequate if you are on a very tight budget or are still working in the experimental and recipe creation phase, but I do not recommend these hand cutters outside of that.

What I do recommend is a good wire cutter explicitly designed for soap loaves or cylinders. There are two main types: single bar cutters and whole loaf cutters. You can get a good single loaf cutter for under 50.00 dollars but keep in mind; you can only cut one bar off your loaf at a time. These single bar cutters are great to start with, but once you sell a good volume of soap, they will quickly become very inefficient for you and quickly outlive their usefulness. Although I no longer use single bar cutters.

Your best and most efficient option is the multi-bar or loaf wire cutter. With this unit, you can cut an entire loaf or cylinder with one motion. One pass and your bars are both smooth and uniform. You can purchase these wire cutters for the thickness of the bar you want to make. The unit I have cuts my bars 1" thick. Although they are relatively expensive, they are well worth the price and I highly recommend buying one. You will save yourself a significant amount of time with these cutters, and time is money, so they quickly pay for themselves.

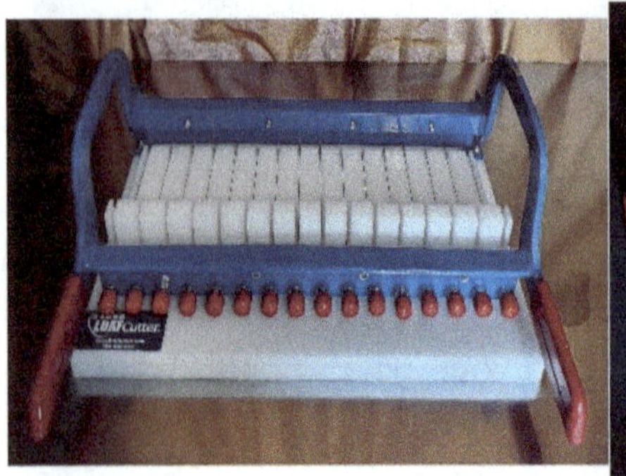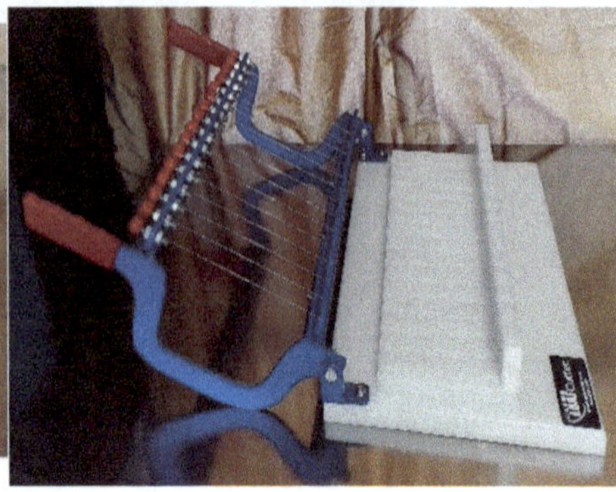

Trimers

If you are going to trim the edges of your bars, you will need trimming tools. Some soapers like me will also cut and trim the top of the bar rather than leaving it rough cut. Trimming a bar on all sides removes the square edge and rounds it. This rounded edge is more comfortable for your customers when they first use your soap. Trimming your soap also gives it a more sculpted professional look.

You can purchase trimming tools explicitly designed for soap from soapmaking supply companies. These trimmers are not worth the money or time. This is one of those areas where you can go cheap. I have experimented with more ways and tools than I can count to trim soap. I have found the best tool is the good old-fashioned carrot peeler. Don't laugh. Carrot peelers work spectacularly well, are easy to use and clean, and give your soap 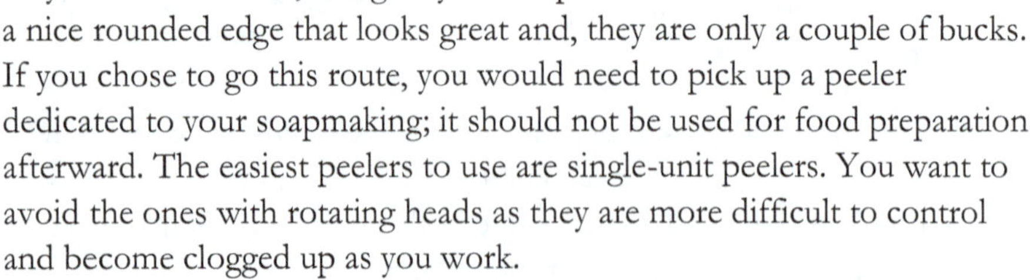 a nice rounded edge that looks great and, they are only a couple of bucks. If you chose to go this route, you would need to pick up a peeler dedicated to your soapmaking; it should not be used for food preparation afterward. The easiest peelers to use are single-unit peelers. You want to avoid the ones with rotating heads as they are more difficult to control and become clogged up as you work.

PACKAGING & LABELS
Preparing Your Soap For The Market

"Packaging can be theater, it can create a story."
—Steve Jobs

WHAT WE WILL LOOK AT IN THIS CHAPTER is the package or wrapper you use for your soap and the label you put on it. For some soapers, the packaging is also the label. As I travel around different farmers and artisan markets, I run across many businesses selling handmade artisan soap. Without fail, there will always be an artisan or two selling their soap with either no package or the soap is wrapped in a small cardboard printed sleeve with 50% to 80% of the soap exposed. Each time I see this, I shudder. Soap is a humectant meaning it absorbs the elements that are around it. Soap that is not protected and wrapped is exposed to people touching it with their dirty hands, coughing on it, sneezing on it, dust from the air, odours from the environment you are in, etc. I would never buy an unwrapped bar of soap, nor will a lot of your potential customers. By not correctly packaging or wrapping your soap, you will lose business. The other negative to not wrapping your soap is your essential oils will dissipate and lose their scent over time. This loss of scent does not happen if you enclose your soap in a package or wrapper. Packaging or wrapping your soap can fall anywhere from complicated and expensive to frugal and easy.

If budget is not an issue and you are looking for an easy way to get your soap packaged, you can go the conventional route, putting your soap into a cardstock box. Most new soapers and even established soapers do not have or will never have the means or expertise to accomplish this in-house, meaning you will have to achieve this through professional packaging companies. The process will start with having a boxboard company design a label for you. A quick google search will point you to companies in your area. You will provide the required information, including,  at a minimum, the size of the soap, company name, logo, address, soap name, ingredients, size, expiry date, warning, and UPC if you use them.

The boxboard company will then print this information on boxes it produces and sells to you. Most companies will have a minimum order requirement.

The other option is to have your artwork professionally created with a graphic artist and provide this print-ready artwork to the box company to produce on the boxes they make for you. This method is costly, takes time, and ties up capital in box inventory. One big plus with this method is your packaging is natural, recyclable, and biodegradable. You will not find many new artisan soapers going to this level. Some do, but they are well established and are now running huge businesses. I would look at this method in the future when your business is flourishing. There are much easier and cheaper ways to get started with your packaging.

One less expensive option I have seen for packaging is purchasing silk, cloth, paper, or burlap bags just a little bigger than the soap bar with drawstrings. Tags are then printed. Most soapers will purchase blank labels and print them on their printer. The printed tags are attached to the bag strings with the required information as above. This method looks good and gets a favourable response from customers, although there is still a fair cost associated with these bags. This method is also recyclable and biodegradable over time as long as you are not using plastic bags. The tags are usually printed in-house. I will address in-house printing and design in a bit.

You can also package your soap by placing it in a shrinkwrap bag, then seal and heat the bag to hug the soap. You can accomplish this easily by purchasing these bags, an inexpensive sealer, and a hairdryer. More extensive operations will buy a machine that does sealing and heat shrinking. You would then either place your sealed soap into a printed sleeve or affix a printed label with the required labelling information. Putting your soap in this type of packaging is a very economical way to package your soap.

The drawback is, your customers will, in some cases, take exception to you using plastics. You can recycle plastic in some places, but it is not biodegradable.

The most economical way to package your soap is to wrap it in a waxed deli wrap and then affix a label that goes around the bar. This label will seal the deli wrap, and your soap will have an artisan professional look to it. This method is the most inexpensive and comes with many advantages. The waxed deli wrap will maintain the scent

of your essential oils and the freshness of your soap for a very long time. Your packaging will be natural and biodegradable. You will have a unique packaging experience for your customers. The method I use to package my soap is this one. The cost of the deli wrap and label I use is 5 cents per bar. Now that's inexpensive packaging that looks great! I receive multiple packaging compliments from both customers and vendors in every market I attend. I highly recommend it.

The above suggestions are just that, suggestions. There are no rules on how you package your soap. I recommend the method I use, but there are many more ways you can accomplish getting your soap into a package. If you don't like any of the above, develop your own. There are no rules except for what information goes on the label or box. If you would like to see what my method looks like, I have created a companion video to see my packaging method in action. You can find it in the reference link that includes a link to the deli wraps and labels I use. It is a slick system.

Once you have determined how you will package your soap, it is time to create your labels. If you have chosen to go with a boxboard package or a printed sleeve, you will have either a graphic artist prepare your label artwork or the boxboard company, and you are all set. You will be unable to accomplish this in-house. As mentioned above, although professional, this is a costly way to go with high upfront costs. I do not recommend it as there are less expensive ways to go that still look great, and remember, every package you need for your new products will have to go through this same process and cost.

What I do recommend is creating your own labels. With today's technology and inexpensive equipment, it is now straightforward and easy to accomplish. Every time you develop a new product, you can create and print your labels for that product and have it ready for the market in a matter of a couple of hours, an incredible advantage to have and a quick way to get your new products out there. For a package, you can choose a generic box, a bag, a wrapper of some type, or shrinkwrap. You will need four items to create a label, a computer, a printer, a graphic arts software program, and stickers to print the label.

To effectively run graphic arts software programs, you need a computer with a little bit of power, or you will spend too much of your time waiting for screen loads, crashes, and graphics to process. I gravitate to Dell Computers and have been using them forever without any issues. They are well built and reasonably priced. If you need a computer or think it is time to upgrade, I have included a medium price point and upper-end model in the resource link at the bottom of the chapter. You will want an i5 or an i7 with a solid state drive (SSD) and at least 8 gigabytes of ram. 16 gigabytes is better. The larger the screen you have, the better for graphics work. If you do have a reasonably powerful computer, you are good to go. If you do not have a sufficiently powerful computer see the links below, or consider hitting the store to upgrade, upgrading will be well worth the cost and effort.

With the advent of Inkjet Ecotank Printers, it is now very economical to print a label in-house. Ecotank Printers no longer use costly ink cartridges. These new printers have ink reservoirs or tanks of the three primary colours, yellow, red, blue, and a reservoir or tank for black. You purchase the ink in large 70ml or 140ml bottles that last for up to 10,000 pages. If you print 6 to 12 labels per sheet, a set of ink bottles can last you for up to 120,000 labels. That's a lot of labels. The cost per label is less than 1 cent or a fraction of a penny for ink and equipment. When you purchase one of these new printers, they come with a full supply of ink that can last six months to a year, depending on how much you are printing. Now that is an inexpensive way to make a label.

These printers cost more than the standard inkjet printer. However, they pay for themselves in a week once you are in production. They come in models that will print a standard 8.5-inch x 11-inch sheet of stickers for around $300.00. You can get larger models that will print sheets up to 14-inches by 18-inches for about $1000.00. These printers will print on photo glossy, gloss, matte, waterproof, and foil labels making for an incredibly professional label. The larger ones will also print double-sided, which is excellent if you will be creating folded handouts or flyers. I own both a small-scale and large-scale model, and they are, without a doubt, the best investment I have ever made. I highly recommend these printers for high production run labelling. I have included these printers in the reference link, along with a companion video if you would like to see them in production.

 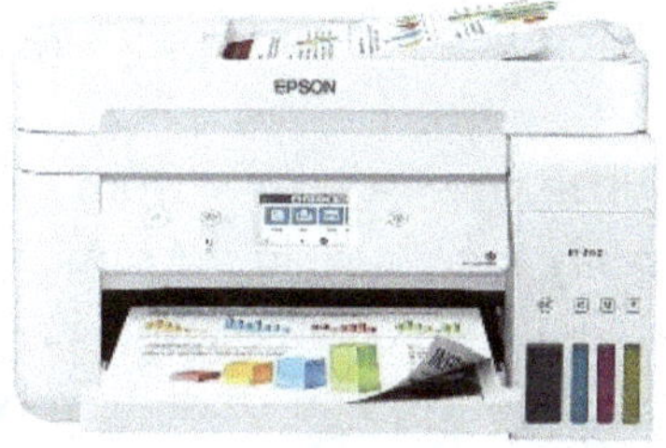

Once you have a printer to print your labels, you will need to create the actual labels. Once again, a straightforward thing to accomplish with the intuitive software available to you today. There are three ways to go with the software—expensive, middle of the road, and free. You will need a software suite that offers two modules, photo editing, and graphic arts. If you already own this software great, you are ready to start making labels. If not, it is decision time. There are two options to purchase software in today's market. One way is to buy a program outright with a one-time payment. The other way is to subscribe to a cloud subscription for an ongoing monthly fee. I have never subscribed to a subscription payment plan for software and never will. I want to pay once and own it. This decision is, of course, up to you.

The most expensive and industry standard for professionals is the adobe suite. The adobe software comes with modules like Photoshop, Illustrator, InDesign, and more. It is costly, over $1,000.00 for the full suite, and has a steep learning curve. Unless you already have the Adobe products or plan to move into graphic art design as one of your business offerings, it is unnecessary to spend this kind of money. I do not recommend this expensive option for our purposes.

The least expensive option is to choose free software. That is pretty cheap. Chuckle. There are many free programs out there you can use to create a label. I have tried most of them, and I hate to say it; I am not a fan for several reasons. The first reason is you have to choose a stand-alone program for each task you want to complete. Your label will have different elements on it, photos, pictures or drawings, and text. Photos and illustrations are manipulated in photo design software, and text or your layout is accomplished in a graphic arts program. When you choose to use free software, you need a software program for each of the tasks you want to achieve. That means learning two or three different pieces of software that different companies or communities have made.

When you use a suite from one company, all the software in that suite generally functions, in the same way, meaning all of the toolbars and buttons are similar. You only have to learn how to work around the programs once. The second problem with free software is it usually has a very steep learning curve, and you will need to spend a lot of time scouring the internet for help files and tutorials. They are not nearly as intuitive as the software suits produced by the more prominent companies.

The third issue with free programs from the larger companies is they will be severely limited in what they can do. You will have to eventually purchase the full program to accomplish all you need to get done. The last and main reason I do not use the free programs is a programming community usually creates them. In time, these communities either disband, discontinue the effort, or stop supporting the product altogether. I have been caught a couple of times with discontinued free software and had to begin again from the very start. As tempting as it is, I don't use or recommend the free software to run a business. If this is your only choice due to budget, I have included the links to some free programs for your photo and graphic arts work in the reference link.

The absolute best option for creating the artwork for your labels if
you do not already own and know how to use the Adobe Suite of
products is the Corel Suite of products. Corel is the lower mid-level
option. You can purchase the complete Corel package for under $200 on
sale. The Corel software package contains CorelDRAW for laying out
and printing your label, Corel PHOTOPAINT for managing your
graphics, and Corel CAPTURE to take
screen cutouts of graphic elements and a
couple of more cool tools. The Corel
software suite is intuitive to learn and has
the best help and tutorial files available.
One of the great options of using Corel is
all the programs look and feel the same.
If you can use one, you can use the
others. If you plan to get into creating
promotional or YouTube videos for your

business, you can also use the Corel program called Pinnacle to make and
edit these videos. This program fits right into the Corel product line's
overall theme and is less than $50 on sale. Corel has been around since
1985, and they have the most extensive worldwide following, so they are
not going to disappear anytime soon. I have confidence in them, and the
Corel Suite is the only set of programs I use. I highly recommend them
for your label creation.

I have created a free Corel video tutorial that will walk you through
the process of creating a label from start to finish. In this tutorial, we will
create one of my labels from concept design, to printing, in about 45
minutes. You can find this tutorial in the reference link in the Appendix.

The last thing you need is the sticker sheets to print your labels. I use
8.5" x 11" sticker sheets that contain the size of the labels I am creating.
One of my soap labels comes on a sheet with six stickers. I purchase
1000 sheets that give me 6000 labels at a time. Depending on the size, a
sheet will come with 2 to sometimes 30 labels per sheet. Using the
method of creating my own labels with CorelDRAW and printing them
out on sticker sheets, my average label cost, as mentioned, is 5 cents per
bar. I live in Canada and import sticker sheets from the US. If you live in
the US, the label per bar would be even cheaper. If you live in other
countries, your cost would be similar to mine. I have searched 100s of

companies to get a reasonably priced box of sticker sheets, and one company beats them all, hands down. The company's name is OnlineLabels.com. You can type this URL into your browser, search for them with your search engine, or find them in the reference link. They have the best prices going by far. I have never seen anything close to their pricing and quality, and no, I do not have any affiliation with this company. They are simply the best.

Following this direction of designing and printing your own labels will have you up and labelling your soap in a very short time with a professional-looking product. Making and printing your own labels is also an excellent method as your business grows. You will be able to create labels as you need them without any delay. The last great reason for creating in-house labels is you will not have to maintain an inventory of preprinted labels for every type of bar of soap you sell. You print your labels as you need them and don't have thousands of dollars tied up in inventory just sitting on a shelf.

MAKING SOAP
Let's Make Some Soap

"Happiness is the secret ingredient for successful businesses. If you have a happy company, it will be invincible."
—Richard Branson

IN THIS CHAPTER WE WILL GET DOWN TO THE BUSINESS of making soap. We will first go through the process of making hot process soap and then cold process soap. Because I do not recommend the hybrid method for all the reasons touched on in the Science of Soap chapter, I will not touch on this method. When you make soap, independent of the process, the first thing you want to do is create a base recipe. A base recipe is a basic set of ingredients you will always use as a starting point for all of your soaps. From this base recipe, you will then add scents and additives to achieve your final product. As an example, you can add lavender essential oil and alkanet powder to your base recipe, and now you have a beautiful purple lavender soap that smells and looks great and so on.

This chapter will provide you with a base starter recipe. From this recipe, you can then create the most spectacular soaps you can imagine. I have gone through over 250 recipe adjustments to arrive at this recipe. When designing a base recipe, you want your soap to exhibit several characteristics. You want it to be hard enough to last as long as a conventional bar of soap. It will need to be moisturizing and conditioning and provide an abundance of bubbly creamy lather, and of course, it will need to be cleansing without drying out the skin. Now that's a tall order. The base recipe I provide has an outstanding balance between each of the desired characteristics. You can also create your own base recipes. How do you do this? Let's start there.

Firstly. each vegetable, nut, fruit oil, or butter you use is a combination of different fatty acids and plant matter. Each fatty acid delivers a different set of characteristics to your soap. Examples of some fatty acids are lauric, linoleic, linolenic, myristic, oleic, palmitic, stearic, and Ricinoleic fatty acids. For instance, Oils high in lauric acid like coconut oil will make a good cleansing, hard bar of soap, with a nice amount of bubbly lather. The drawback of this fatty acid is your soap will be super drying to the skin with minimal moisturizing and conditioning properties.

For this reason, soapers don't make their soap with only one oil. They mix oils and butters to balance all the desired properties they seek to accomplish in their soap. A great bar of soap includes several oils, butters, and additives to achieve perfection. One example of an additive is kaolin clay. This clay helps to draw out toxins and provides slip and glide over the skin. Each oil, butter, or animal fat has what is called a saponification value. This value is how many oil, butter, or animal fat units are required to saponify one unit of lye. We will discuss this in a sec.

Your second component is your chosen liquid. It can either impart desired characteristics to your soap or, like water, be mixed with lye to provide the catalyst to begin the saponification process. When using water, I highly recommend you use distilled water only. Tap water is full of chlorine, calcium, and minerals that you do not want in your soap. Well, and spring water is full of calcium, minerals, and other contaminants you do not want in your soap. I use filtered rainwater that I filter twice, and then I run it through ceramic filters giving me purity of 99.7%. If you are using milk, or juice you should dilute these liquids with 30% water. You first mix your lye into your water, then mix the lye solution into the other liquid. This way, you get all of your lye well mixed. For example, If you combine your lye directly with milk, it will begin to saponify from the milk's fat. If you mix your lye with water and then add this lye/water into your milk, you will not get premature saponification before mixing this combined solution into your oils. You will need to make beer, wine, or spirits "flat" by gently simmering them over heat to remove the alcohol content. Milk will give you a very creamy moisturizing bar of soap. Juices, beer, and wine will provide you with a very bubbly bar of soap with lots of lather due to the sugars in them.

The third component of your soap is the lye. Lye is known as sodium hydroxide, caustic soda, or pearl ash. When purchasing lye, you want to avoid buying it at your local hardware store. The lye from hardware stores is not certified pure or clean, even if it says pure on the label. You want your lye to be at a minimum purity of 99%. It is best to buy it from your local soap supply company. When mixing lye with your liquid, you always add it to the liquid slowly while stirring under ventilation or outdoors. Never add your liquid to the lye. When you mix lye with a liquid, it heats up rapidly. If you add your liquid to the lye, your lye can volcano out of your mixing bowl. Always add lye to your liquid, never the other way around.

Always wear your safety gear when mixing lye and your liquid or your lye solution into your oils. Your safety gear should consist of latex or rubber gloves and a full face mask, closed-toe shoes, an old long-sleeved shirt and old pants, and a smock. You should also have an emergency eyewash station close to your lye mixing area. Never leave your lye solution unattended or in the vicinity of people that are not involved in the process of making the soap, children, or pets. Handled safely and under controlled conditions with your full safety gear, there should be no issue or concern working with lye.

When working with lye, you always want to have a spray bottle of 100% white vinegar close to the mixing station and a bowl with a diluted 50-50 mixture of vinegar and water with a cloth soaking in it. Once you finish all your mixing, you can store this solution until next time. Vinegar neutralizes lye. If you spill or splash any lye solution on your skin, immediately neutralize it with the vinegar and then wash and soak the area for 15 minutes with soap and water. If you spill any lye solution around your work area or on your clothes or shoes, neutralize it with your vinegar spritzer and clean it up immediately. If you do receive a burn from lye, seek medical attention.

Creating Recipies

You will be dealing with oils, butters, fats, lye, water, milk, additives, and rules. That's a lot to take in. The good news is, you don't have to learn what oils have what fatty acids in them, or what characteristics those fatty acids have, or what their saponification values are. You don't have to calculate by hand what percentages of what oils give you the characteristics you are seeking because there are several online tools out there that do it for you with great clarity. Of course, you can manually do these calculations, but why recreate the wheel when the tools available do the job just fine.

There are two options; a stand-alone program like Soapmaker 3 or an online soap calculator. You use these calculators to create your recipes. One significant advantage of the software called SoapMaker 3 is in addition to developing recipes, you can also track shipments and inventory, the cost of a batch and a bar of your soap, orders, sales, and create invoices. This is the program I use today, and I highly recommend it. I will go over this program after we look at the online calculator. When I first started, I used online calculators to create my recipes, and they work fine. You can find many soap calculators on the internet, and many soap supply companies offer them. The one I find most comfortable to use is SoapCalc, located at www.soapcalc.net. You can either click on this URL if reading this as an ebook or enter it onto your browser if reading the paperback version. Once on the main page:

At the top of the page, left-click on the menu that says "Recipe Calculator."

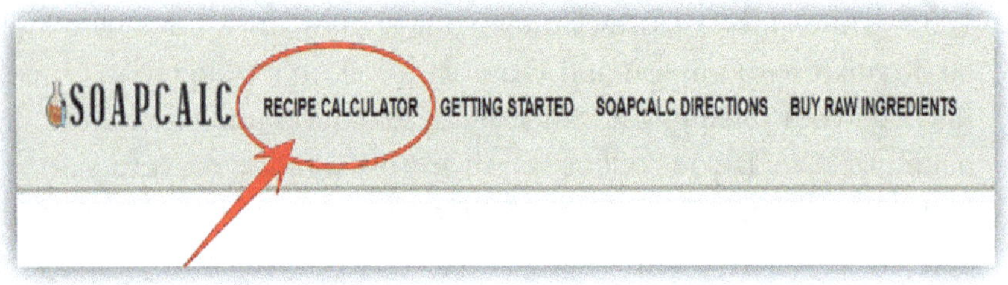

Image 1

Once the calculator is opened you will see this page.

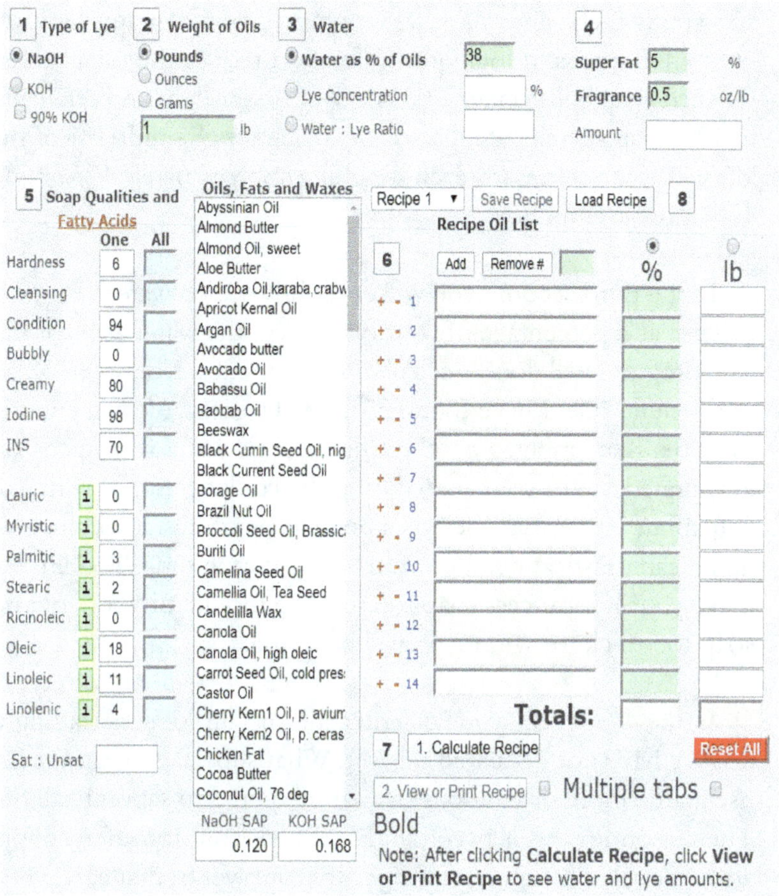

Image 2

You will enter all of your information here on this page. Let's go through section by section and see what we have. As I am going through the sections, I will create the basic base recipe I will be showing you through this chapter.

In the top section, you will first enter the type of lye you will be using. For bar soap, we use sodium hydroxide, chemically known as NaOH. Select the NaOH button.

In the second section, you will enter your weight of oils. I use grams. This example will be in grams, so select the grams button. To easily calculate your oil weight, multiply the number of bars you will be making by the weight per finished cured bar. For our example, I will use 4 bars at 125 grams each. The oils' total weight will be 500 grams less 10%. 500 x .90 = 450 grams of total oils. Why did I reduce the total by 10%? Your finished soap will contain 100% of your oil weight and retain about 10% to 12% water once cured. Your oils' total weight and 10% of the water left will give you 4 bars, each weighing approximately 125 grams. Enter 450 in the second box.

In the third section, you will enter how much water or total liquid you will use as a percentage of your oils. Select the water as % of oils button. The program will do this calculation. Soapers use between 32% and 38% as a general rule. I have found 35% works great. We will enter 35% in this box. Remember, a good portion of this water will be cooked or evaporated out of your soap during the cooking and or curing, leaving you about 10% to 12% left as a percentage of oils. Too much water or liquid can drastically extend your soap's curing time. Too little water will make your hot process soap too thick to mould, or your cold process soap too thick to swirl if you will be swirling.

In the 4th section, you will enter the amount of superfatting you will do. We have not discussed this yet. What superfatting means is you will use a little more of your oils than are required to saponify all of your lye. The reason for this is two-fold. Firstly, we do it for safety. Suppose you add precisely enough oils to saponify your lye. In that case, you risk having chemically hot soap, meaning you will possibly have lye left in your soap or lye that has not saponified. Soap with lye left in it called chemically hot Soap. Chemically hot soap can burn you. This can happen for a couple of reasons, your scales are not exact or do not measure to the tenth of a gram, or you have not gotten every drop of oil out of your measuring containers. We avoid this by adding a little extra oil. Secondly, having a little extra oil in your soap helps to make your soap more moisturizing—Soapers superfat between 2% and 10%. I superfat at 4 %. Too much superfatting will make your soap too soft. Enter 4% in this box. Some soapers will save their exotic oils to the end for the superfatting and add the 4% extra after they have brought their soap to trace. With this method, your more exotic oils remain in the soap in their pure form for moisturizing.

The last section below your superfatting box is your fragrance or essential oils. The program calculates fragrance as to how many grams per kilogram of soap. I like to scent at 3%. The program calculates g/kg. There are 1000 grams in a kilogram. To scent at 3%, multiply 1000 by 3%, and you get 30. 30 would be the entry for the fragrance box. Suppose you want to scent at a different percentage; multiply 1000 by that percentage. Our example will calculate out to 13.5 grams of essential oil, which is 3% of 450 grams, the batch weight we are using.

The below graphic shows you what the program's top section should look like when filled in as above. If you are following along in the online calculator, go ahead and make the selections and fill in the numbers.

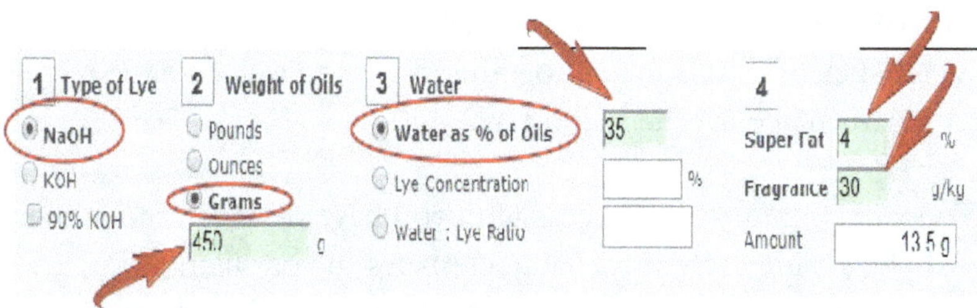

Image 3

Section 5 and section 6 is where the action happens. You will see six soap characteristics: hardness, cleansing, condition, bubbly, creamy, iodine, and INS. If you hover over each one, you will get a range considered acceptable for your soap. For example, you want to achieve a hardness score between 29 and 54.

Below the characteristics, you will see the fatty acid profile. If you hover your mouse over the fatty acid, the fatty acid's information will be provided. If you click on the i in the green box to the right, an information page for that fatty acid will open. Remember, each oil or butter you choose for your soap comprises a combination of these fatty acids, glycerin and plant matter.

On the right-hand side, you will see the list of oils, butters and some additives. You will design your recipe out of a combination of these. When you select an individual ingredient on the right, it will populate the characteristics, and fatty acid profile on the left, showing them in the column of small boxes labelled "One" for that particular oil. When you double-click the oil, it will place it in section 6 on the page's right-hand side. Once your selected oil is in the right-hand column, choose the button for either how many grams you will be using out of 450 grams or what percentage of the total recipe this oil will be. If you enter by weight, all the oils entered will need to add up to 450 grams for our example or the total weight of oils you have selected as a weight. When you enter by the percentage of oil, you need to reach 100%. I use percentages. Next, choose a second ingredient from the right-hand column and double-click it. This 2nd oil is added to the column of ingredients on the right, and the column of small boxes on the left labelled "All" will give you the characteristics of all oils mixed together once you calculate the recipe. Enter a percentage for the second oil.

You will continue this process until you have designed the perfect bar of soap, balancing each of the characteristics to your liking. If you want to remove an ingredient from the column on the right side of the page, there is a little minus sign (-) on the ingredient's left-hand side. Clicking this minus sign will remove it. There is also a small plus sign(+) there you can use to add a selected oil individually.

You can save up to 8 recipes. To save a recipe, select the box that says recipe 1, choose a number from 1 to 8 and then click the save button beside it. You load a recipe by selecting the recipe number and clicking the load recipe button.

When your recipe is complete, at box number 7, you will click the "Calculate Recipe" button and then select the "View or Print Recipe" button below it. Your completed recipe will pop up for printing or viewing. The below graphic shows the entries for the example recipe we are using. If you follow along online with SoapCalc, go ahead and make all the entries into the soap calculator that I have and then click the "Calculate Recipe" button. Your screen should look like the screenshot below.

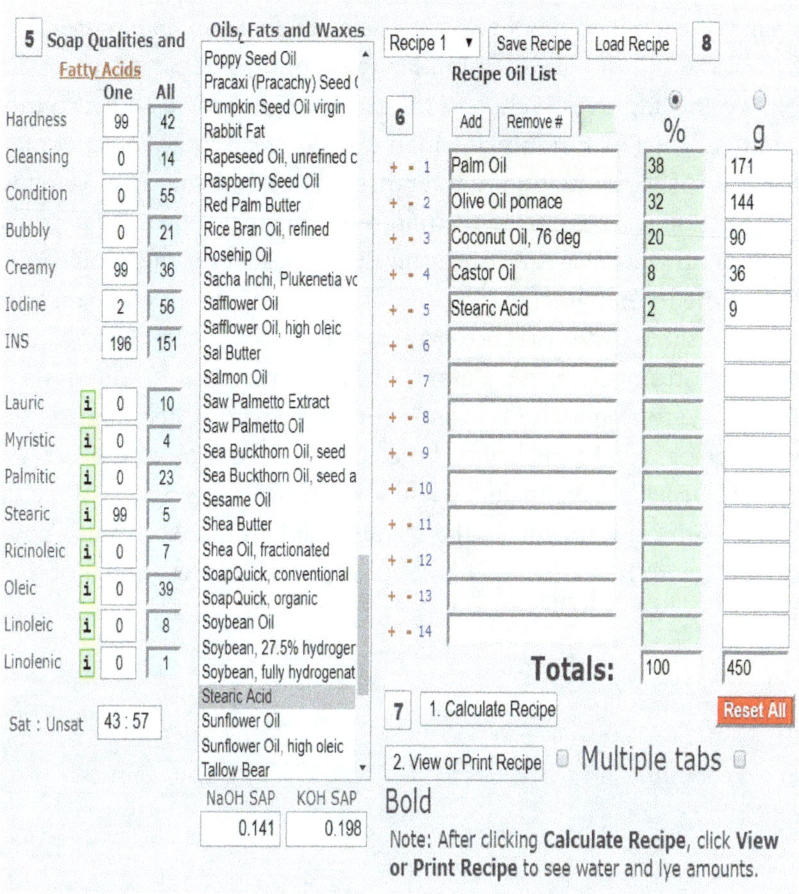

Image 4

You will play with different ingredients adding and subtracting them in different percentages until you have designed the perfect balance of characteristics you want in your soap. As you become more educated with what oils deliver what characteristics, there will be less trial and error. You will be able to hone in on your ingredients quicker. As mentioned, I have designed two base recipes—the basic one above and a premium one that I will share in a bit.

Once you are happy with your recipe, go ahead and click the "View or Print Recipe" button located just below the "Calculate Recipe" button.

The graphic below, or, if you are following along in SoapCalc, is the final recipe you will print. The recipe includes the ingredient weight in grams of each ingredient you will use to make your soap, water, lye fragrance, and the oils of palm, olive, coconut, and castor with steric acid. Notice the additives section at the bottom left. I have added to the additives section 4 grams of kaolin clay, ¼ teaspoon of alkanet powder for a purple colour, and the fragrance will be 13.5 grams of lavender essential oil. I have circled them in red. This recipe now gives you a section on your characteristics and the fatty acid profile. You can name the recipe in the "Recipe Name" box at the top and include additives and notes in the bottom two boxes. You can hit the "Show Graph" button on the bottom left to see a graph of the characteristics. There is a print link at the top right and bottom right of the page. Click this link to print your recipe. If this has been a little confusing for you or you are a more visual learner, I have included a video tutorial on using SoapCalc. You can find the link for this in the resource link in the Appendix. You are now ready to make soap. This recipe size makes a test batch of 4, 125 g bars.

SoapCalc ©	Recipe Name:	Base Recipe - Lavender Soap		New	INCI Names	Print Recipe

Total oil weight	450 g	Sat : Unsat Ratio	43 : 57
Water as percent of oil weight	**35.00 %**	Iodine	56
Super Fat/Discount	4 %	INS	151
Lye Concentration	28.672 %	Fragrance Ratio	30
Water : Lye Ratio	2.4877:1	Fragrance Weight	13.50 g

	Pounds	Ounces	Grams
Water	0.347	5.56	157.50
Lye - **NaOH**	0.140	2.23	63.31
Oils	0.992	15.87	450.00
Fragrance	0.030	0.48	13.50
Soap weight before CP cure or HP cook	1.509	24.14	684.31

#	√	Oil/Fat	%	Pounds	Ounces	Grams
1		Palm Oil	38.00	0.377	6.03	171.00
2		Olive Oil pomace	32.00	0.317	5.08	144.00
3		Coconut Oil, 76 deg	20.00	0.198	3.17	90.00
4		Castor Oil	8.00	0.079	1.27	36.00
5		Stearic Acid	2.00	0.020	0.32	9.00
		Totals	100.00	0.992	15.87	450.00

Soap Bar Quality	Range	Your Recipe		
Hardness	29 - 54	42	Lauric	10
Cleansing	12 - 22	14	Myristic	4
Conditioning	44 - 69	55	Palmitic	23
Bubbly	14 - 46	21	Stearic	5
Creamy	16 - 48	36	Ricinoleic	7
Iodine	41 - 70	56	Oleic	39
INS	136 - 165	151	Linoleic	8
			Linolenic	1

Additives	Notes
4g Kaolin Clay 13.5g Lavender Essential Oil 1/4 Teaspoon of alkanet Powder	

Image 5

SoapCalc, and the included base recipe, is a good starting point for you to begin making soap. You can use this recipe as a springboard to create your own unique formulas with scents, additives, and colours. Even though the base recipe will not change, each of your final product creations can be unique and specific to your business and brand. You can find many recipes on the internet, but if you choose to copy what others have made, your product and your business will not be unique to you. As you gain experience, you will experiment with making your own unique base recipes. I run into many soapers in my travels, all making the same soap from the same internet recipe. I will discourage you from becoming an internet warrior in this area. Be creative; create uniquely spectacular soaps that are yours for your customers. The next chapter will cover scents, additives, and colouring your soap. Now that we have a recipe to work from, let's make some soap. I will assume we are using the sample recipe above. If you will be working with your own recipe, substitute your ingredients and quantities for the ones listed.

Making Lavender Hot Process Soap (Detailed step by step instructions)

Step One – Preparing to make a batch of soap. Your first step is to prepare your soap studio for the production run. You will want to make sure you are wearing the appropriate clothes for mixing lye and that you put on your latex or rubber gloves, your hairnet, and your smock. Place your safety goggles or face mask, your white vinegar spray bottle, and 50-50 white vinegar/water solution and cloth beside your lye station to be ready for use. Check to make sure your scales are clean and that your scales and thermometers are in good working shape. Replace any batteries if necessary. Ensure your eyewash station is ready for any potential emergency, and your fire extinguisher is registering in the green and available for use if needed. Secure your soap studio from children, pets, and anyone not involved in making the soap.

Step Two – Place one 1-cup measuring cup and one 2-cup measuring cup out by your lye station with a whisk and a thermometer. Set up a large and small scale at your oils mixing station with one 4-cup measuring cup and three small glass bowls with a spatula and a large and small stainless steel spoon. Place your CrockPot bowl or heating pot at your oils mixing station. Set a thermometer at your oils mixing station. Set a spray bottle of 99% proof isopropyl alcohol at your oils mixing station.

Step Three – Place your lye and a bottle of distilled water at the lye mixing station. Place your palm oil, olive oil, coconut oil, castor oil, kaolin clay, lavender essential oil, alkanet powder, and stearic acid at your oils mixing station.

Step Four – If using a loaf or cylinder mould, line the mould with parchment, wax, or freezer paper. Gently spritz the inside of the lined mould with your 99% proof isopropyl alcohol and set the mould aside. If you are using a silicone mould, spritz it with your 99% proof isopropyl alcohol and set it aside. Now lightly spritz your utensils, pot, measuring cups, glass bowls, gloves, and work surfaces with isopropyl alcohol. Let this alcohol spritz sit for about two minutes, then dry everything with a paper towel. Most items will already be dry due to the alcohol evaporating. If you wait long enough, the alcohol will evaporate on its own. Not many soapers sterilize before a production run, but I highly recommend you do this for a couple of reasons. You are guaranteeing you do not transfer any germs or bacteria into your raw materials, helping to preserve them for their full life-cycle, and it is an excellent habit to develop. Once you move into the water in oil or oil in water products, you will have to sterilize everything. These types of products, like hand creams, need to be produced in a 100% germ and bacteria-free environment to prevent moulding. Develop the habit now, and it will become a natural routine you follow without thinking.

Step Five – It is time to measure out all your ingredients. Before you begin measuring, make sure you have enough of each raw material. Setting all materials out at the beginning of production allows you to visually inspect everything to ensure you have enough of each item. Confirming your ingredients before mixing is a best practice and an excellent habit to follow. Make it part of your regular routine when making soap. If you have any concerns that you might be even a little short of something, weigh it to make sure. Once you start heating, things are now on a timeline, and you won't have time to track down missing materials.

Go to your lye station, put on your safety mask and make sure your gloves are on. Turn your large scale on, then place the 1-cup measuring cup on the scale and push the tare button on your scale. Taring the scale resets the scale to zero with the measuring cup on it. Weigh 63.30 grams of lye into the measuring cup. You will notice our recipe calls for 63.31 grams of lye. Your scale will only measure down to one-tenth of a gram, so we cant get the .01 in there. Always round down when it comes to lye and always round up when it comes to oils and additives for safety reasons to ensure we never end up with lye heavy soap. In this case, we have rounded down from 63.31 to 63.30. Remove the measuring cup and place the 2-cup measuring cup on the scale and tare it. Weigh out 157.50 grams of distilled water into this measuring cup. Set both of these aside at your lye mixing station.

Go to your oils mixing station, turn on your large scale and then place the 4-cup measuring cup on the scale. Tare the scale, then add 171 grams of palm oil. Leave the measuring cup on the scale and tare it again. Your scale will now read zero even though you have the measuring cup with palm oil on the scale. Now add 144 grams of palm oil and tare the scale again. Add 90 grams of coconut oil and tare the scale one last time and add the 36 grams of castor oil. Set the measuring cup full of palm, olive, coconut, and castor oils aside.

Get out your small scale and turn it on. Place one of your small glass bowls on the scale and push the tare button. Add 4 grams of kaolin clay and ¼ of a teaspoon of the alkanet powder to the clay. Move this small glass bowl over to your lye mixing station and place it beside your lye and water that are already there. Place a second glass bowl on the scale and tare it. Add 9 grams of stearic acid to the glass bowl and set it aside. Put your last small glass bowl on your scale and tare it. Add 13.5 grams of lavender essential oil to this bowl. Remove it from the scale, cover the top with plastic wrap, and then set an item on the top of the bowl like cardboard or paper to protect it from the light. Essential oils are light-sensitive. You want to protect the integrity of the oils. You are now ready to start cooking your soap batch.

Step Six – Put the palm, olive, coconut, and castor oils from your 4-cup measuring cup into your crockpot bowl. Add the stearic acid to the CrockPot bowl and place the bowl into the CrockPot heating unit. Place the lid on your crockpot and turn it on to low. While your oils are heating, set one of your thermometers, your stick blender, a silicone spoon, and your phenolphthalein at your cooking station. (I will discuss phenolphthalein and PH at the end of the chapter). Once your coconut and palm oils are close to being melted, stir your pot every 10 minutes or so until your temperature reaches 130 degrees Fahrenheit. Stirring the oils helps to mix in the stearic acid properly. When your oils reach 130 degrees Fahrenheit, turn the CrockPot off and leave the lid on the pot.

Step Seven- Head over to your lye station, put your face mask on, and turn on your ventilation. If you do not have ventilation move the ingredients and your whisk to a safe outside location. You never want to inhale the gasses produced when mixing lye with water. Slowly pour your lye into the water while mixing with your whisk. Never pour your water into your lye. As you mix your lye into the water, your solution will turn cloudy and start to heat up rapidly. If your water is at an average room temperature, your mixture will heat between 180 and 200 degrees

Fahrenheit. Continue stirring until the solution becomes clear. Once your solution is clear, whisk in the clay and alkanet powder. Your solution will now turn purple. Move this combined solution to your cooking station and place it close to your CrockPot. Now you will wait until both your oils and your water/lye solution cool to between 110 and 125 degrees Fahrenheit. This temperature range is the ideal range to mix your oils and lye solution together. Never mix your ingredients if they are higher than 125 degrees Fahrenheit. Doing so can cause your mixture to volcano up and out of the pot. I also recommend that you never mix your ingredients under 110 degrees Farenheight as this will throw your average cooking times off and affect how long it takes to bring your mixture to trace. As you wait for your solutions to cool, you can begin some of the clean-up.

Step Eight – Once your oils and your lye/water solution are both in the range of 110 to 125 degrees Fahrenheit, put your face mask back on and turn your CrockPot back on to low. Place your stick blender into your oils. Do this by inserting it at an angle. You do not want any air caught in the bottom of the blender. Run your blender on the low setting to give your oils and stearic acid a good mixing. Give your lye/water solution a good stir with the whisk as the clay will have settled on the measuring cup's bottom. With your stick blender on low, slowly pour your lye/water solution into your oils, being careful not to splash any outside of your pot. Now you will stick blend the combined solution through to heavy trace. Keep moving your stick blender around the pot, making sure not to let the blades come out of the mixture. Change your blender speed between low and high periodically. You will know you have reached a heavy trace when you lift your stick blender out of the mixture, and the ridge created by this action does not sink back into the mixture. Make sure you have turned your stick blender off when you lift it out to test for trace. This process should take 5 to 10 minutes for this recipe. Once you have reached a heavy trace, lift your stick blender out of your mixture, scrap the soap off the bottom of the blender back into the pot. Remove your stick blender and place it in your empty 4-cup measuring cup along with your whisk. Run your spatula along the inside of the pot, removing any soap close to the edge. Moving this soap away from the pot's upper sides prevents it from burning during the cooking process. Move this soap to the center of the pot. Take the measuring cup, spatula, whisk, and blender bottom to your cleaning station. Cover your pot with plastic wrap. Plastic wrap does a better job of keeping the moisture in the pot than the lid does. Poke a couple of small holes in the plastic wrap to help release pressure in your pot as your soap cooks. Record the time you cover your CrockPot with plastic wrap. Go to your cleaning station and spritz the measuring cup, blender bottom, and utensils with your white vinegar solution. Rinse and wash everything with soap and water. Once clean, return your spatula to your cooking station.

Step Nine – Cook your soap for precisely one hour on low. Do not remove the plastic wrap or interrupt this cooking time. As your soap cooks, it will go through stages. (take my word for it, don't remove the plastic wrap) First, it will become hard and impossible to stir. Shortly after that, you will see the soap start to curl up from the edges and into the center of the pot. After that, a liquid will begin to appear in the center of the pot. This pool of liquid is glycerin separating as your soap is going through the saponification process. Once you see a beautiful pool of glycerin, your hour should be up. Once the hour is up, remove the plastic wrap and discard it.

Put your face shield and gloves back on and give the soap a good stir with your spatula. You want to make sure the glycerin is stirred back into the soap. Some soapers will tell you not to disturb your soap until complete. I can't entirely agree with this. CrockPots cook from the outside-in. Your soap will be very hot on the bottom and the edges and much cooler or uncooked in the center. By stirring, you are redistributing the heat through the whole batch. Stirring ensures all your oils and lye are being saponified through the balance of the cook. Place another sheet of plastic wrap over the pot and cook for an additional 25 minutes. After 25 minutes, remove the plastic wrap, turn the pot off and stir the soap well. It is now done and should look and feel like mashed potatoes.

Step Ten – It is now time to test your soap to make sure it is not lye heavy. Please be aware; we are not testing for a PH level. You can only test for an accurate PH level in an aqueous solution using a PH meter. We are testing to ensure the soap has no lye left in it. Our recipe is designed to ensure all lye will be saponified, providing you have correctly weighed your ingredients, you have brought your soap to trace, you have fully cooked the soap, and your scales are working. (Please see the notes at the end of the chapter to learn about PH testing.) With your clean spatula, smear a tiny bit of soap on a paper towel from the center of the pot. Repeat this process from both ends of the pot. Now drip a couple of drops of phenolphthalein on each smear. If the smears remain clear or you see a very light pink colour, your soap is complete and between 8 to 10 PH for this recipe. If your soap smears turn mid to vivid pink, there is a problem. Either your soap has not cooked long enough, or there was a mistake in the ingredients, or your scales are not accurate. If only one of your smears turns a mid to vivid pink, you did not stir your soap well enough at your first stir and will need to cook it a little longer. I recommend this safety test. If there were human or mechanical errors, you would know about them. If your soap did turn mid to vivid pink, you can try cooking it for another half an hour and repeat the test. If it is now ok, great, otherwise the batch will need to be discarded. Some soapers will suggest adding more oils or a neutralizer like citric acid to complete the soap with further cooking. I disagree with attempting to fix a bad batch because now you are guessing where you went wrong. Even if you were able to save it, your finished product would not have the same characteristics as all your other soaps due to the addition of oils added out of proportion.

Step Eleven – If your soap has tested clear or with a slight pink tinge, remove the pot from the cooking unit and place it at your moulding station. Turn your CrockPot off. Let the soap cool to 140 to 145 degrees Fahrenheit, stirring every 10 minutes. Once you reach somewhere between these temperatures, mix your lavender essential oil with a silicone spoon into your soap batter. Mix this oil in very well. If you attempt to incorporate the essential oil into your soap at a higher temperature than 145 degrees Fahrenheit, you will burn off some essential oil and damage it. Once your oil is mixed in well, start to spoon the soap into your mould in three stages: a bottom layer, a mid-layer, and a top layer. Your soap should have the texture of mashed potatoes. Give the mould 7 or 8 good bangs on the table after filling each layer to remove the air bubbles and settle the soap. Once the mould is full, lightly spritz with 99% proof rubbing alcohol and cover the mould with plastic wrap. Once you cover the mould, give the soap a pat-down with your hand and then set it aside overnight to set up. Your soap is complete and ready for cutting into bars in the morning. Scrape the edges of the pot from excess soap. I pat this extra soap into a small bar and use it for my personal stock. You can use this soap immediately. Clean your work area and everything you have used for the cook and put everything back in its spot ready for your next cook.

Step Twelve – The morning after your soap cook, remove the soap from the mould and cut it into bars. Do not extend the cutting of the soap past one day, or it will become too hard to use a wire cutter. Once the soap is in bars, trim it to your satisfaction and set it aside to cure for one week. During this week, each bar will lose 10 to 15% of its weight in water. After the week, you are ready to package and label your soap and send it to the market. Congratulations if this was your first hot process soap cook.

Making Lavender Cold Process Soap (Detailed step by step instructions)

Step One – Complete steps one to five listed above under "Making Lavender Hot Process Soap."

Step Six – Put the palm, olive, coconut, and castor oils from your 4-cup measuring cup into your stainless steel cooking pot. Add the stearic acid to the pot and place the pot into your induction stove. Place the lid on your pot and turn it on to 180 degrees Fahrenheit. While your oils are heating, set one of your thermometers, your stick blender, a silicone spoon, and your phenolphthalein at your cooking station. (I will discuss phenolphthalein and PH at the end of the chapter). Once your coconut and palm oils are close to being melted, stir your pot every 10 minutes or so until your temperature reaches 130 degrees Fahrenheit. Stirring the oils helps to mix in the stearic acid properly. When your oils reach 145 degrees Fahrenheit, turn the stove off and leave the lid on the pot.

Step Seven- Head over to your lye station, put your face mask on, and turn on your ventilation. If you do not have ventilation move the ingredients and your whisk to a safe outside location. You never want to inhale the gasses produced when mixing lye with water. Slowly pour your lye into the water while mixing with your whisk. Never pour your water into your lye. As you mix your lye into the water, your solution will turn cloudy and start to heat up rapidly. If your water is at an average room temperature, your mixture will heat to between 180 and 200 degrees Fahrenheit. Continue stirring until the solution becomes clear. Once your solution is clear, whisk in the clay and alkanet powder. Your solution will now turn purple. Move this combined solution to your cooking station and place it close to your pot of heated oils. Now you will wait until both your oils and your water/lye solution cool to between 110 and 125 degrees Fahrenheit. This temperature range is the ideal range to mix your oils and lye solution together. As you wait for your solutions to cool, you can begin some of the clean-up.

Step Eight – Once your oils and your lye/water solution are both in the range of 110 to 125 degrees Fahrenheit, put your face mask back on and remove your pot of oils from the stove. Place your stick blender into the oils in your pot. Do this by inserting it at an angle. You do not want any air caught in the bottom of the blender. Run your blender on the low setting to give your oils and stearic acid a good mixing. Give your lye/water solution a good stir with the whisk as the clay will have settled on the measuring cup's bottom. With your stick blender on low, slowly pour your lye/water solution into your oils, being careful not to splash any outside of your pot. Now you will stick blend the combined solution through to heavy trace. Keep moving your stick blender around the pot, making sure not to let the blades come out of the mixture. Change your blender speed between low and high periodically. You will know you have reached a light trace when you lift your stick blender out of the mixture, and the ridge created by this action slowly sinks back into the mixture. Make sure you have turned your stick blender off when you lift it out to test for trace. This process should take 5 to 10 minutes for this recipe. Once you have reached a light trace, lift your stick blender out of your mixture, scrap the soap off the bottom of the blender back into the pot. Remove your stick blender and place it in your empty 4-cup measuring cup along with your whisk. Take the measuring cup, whisk, and blender bottom to your cleaning station.

Step Nine – Place your mould beside your saponified soap pot. Make sure your face shield is still secure, then pour the soap into your mould. Spatula the sides of the pot to get all the soap. Take your pot and spatula to the cleaning area. Return to your mould and gently tap it on the table 7 to 8 times to level the soap. Be careful not to splash the soap out of the mould. Now spritz the top of the mould with 99% isopropyl alcohol and cover with plastic wrap. Set the mould in your curring area for three days. With cold process soap, soda ash can develop on the loaf's top during the curing process. The reason for the alcohol and wrap is to prevent this.

Soda ash does not harm your soap, it can be scraped off, but it is easier to avoid it.

Step Ten – After three days, remove your soap from the mould and cut it into bars. Make sure you wear your safety gloves. The soap will be chemically hot or not yet fully saponified. Once the bars are cut, trim the edges and set the bars aside to cure for five to six weeks. During this curing process, it will fully saponify. Test your soap for lye by shaving a small piece off the center of a bar. Heat the shaving in a microwave for 10 seconds and then wet it with a bit of water and mix it into the soap. Place the wet shaving in a paper towel and apply two drops of phenolphthalein to the soap. If it remains clear or has a very slight pink tinge, it is good to go. If the soap exhibits a mid to vivid pink, it needs to cure longer. If the soap remains mid to bright pink, the batch is no good. Discard the batch safely. Once saponified, it is ready for labeling and packaging. Your soap is now ready for the market. Congratulations if this was your first cold process soap cook.

Tips and Tricks

1. If you would like your hot process soap to look less rustic, you can increase your percentage of water in the batch. Although this is fine, it will take longer for your soap to cure. Do not increase the water content for cold process soap. It is not necessary. Never adjust oil or lye percentages unless first run through a soap calculator

2. If you want to have swirls, a design, or layers in your soap, make two half batches or four quarter batches of different colours simultaneously. Pour one layer at a time into your mould for layers. For swirls or a design, pour the smaller batches side by side into the mould. Use a fork or a chopstick to swirl the soap around the mould. Be artistic. There are no rules. Swirling and layering work well with cold process soap. You can swirl and layer with hot process soap, but the outcome will be choppy.

3. If you want ridges or a ruffled top on the top of your soap, you can form these ridges or ruffles after pouring your soap into the mould. Use a spatula to make ridges to your liking. Ridges work well with both the hot and cold process methods.

4. If you would like to have embedded designs in your soap, cut a cured different colour bar of soap into shapes of your choice and push these shapes into the mould as soon as you pour your soap. Your soap will cure around these embedded soap shapes. This method works best with cold process soap.

5. If you would like to speed up the curing process of hot process soap, place the soap in a small room with a dehumidifier. The cure time will reduce by one to two weeks

6. If you would like to increase the cure time of cold process soap, place the soap in a room with a temperature of at least 85 degrees with a dehumidifier. Heat speeds up the saponification process. You can cut one to two weeks off your curing time.

7. To easily clean your equipment and utensils after a hot process cook, make sure everything that came in contact with lye was spritzed with white vinegar and rinsed. Then fill your crockpot bowl with water. Place all your measuring cups, utensils, and blender bottom in the CrockPot bowl and let it soak for a couple of hours. After a couple of hours, the soap will dissolve, making it easy to rinse and wash.

8. To easily clean your equipment and utensils after a cold process cook, Place all your measuring cups, utensils, and blender bottom in the pot. Fill your cooking pot with 1 cup of white vinegar and the rest of the pot with water. After a couple of hours, the soap will dissolve and neutralize, making it easy to rinse and wash everything.

Note on Creating Recipies

I mentioned an excellent program to create recipes, track deliveries, track inventory of raw materials and finished goods, soap costing, and more. This program is called SoapMaker 3. It is a beautiful program and the one I use. I no longer use online soap calculators. I will not cover it in this book, but I have created a tutorial video if you would like to learn about this program and see it in action. You can find this free video in the resource link in the Appendix.

Note on PH testing

To ensure you do not have lye-heavy soap, you need to make sure several things have happened. Firstly, create your recipe within a soap calculator with a minimum superfat of 4%. Secondly, ensure you measure all ingredients by weight to the 10th of a gram, and your scales are accurate. Thirdly, cook or cure your soap for the prescribed time. If you have done all of this, you will never have lye-heavy soap. We test our soap to make sure there was no human or mechanical error from the above list.

There is only one way to take an actual accurate PH measurement of your soap. PH can only be measured accurately in an aqueous solution using and following PH meter directions. These are expensive scientific pieces of equipment. I have never run across another soaper that tests every batch with one of these meters. I have a PH meter but only use it to confirm that my phenolphthalein testing process is adequate to ensure my soap is not lye-heavy.

There are many people out there providing false or dangerous information on PH testing. I agree we need to test our soap to ensure we have not made an error as above, but the test cannot predict PH. It is to verify that our soap is within a PH range. If we have followed all directions and processes, our soap will be, on average, in the 8 to 10 PH range.

PH testing strips are useless. You can use seven different strips and get seven very different readings, even using the same manufacturer's strips. I think these are a big waste of time.

Some soaper will zap test their soap. Zap testing is sticking the tip of your tongue on the bar of soap to see if you get a zap, like sticking your tongue on a battery terminal. If you get a zap, your soap is lye-heavy. No, I am not kidding. There are people out there doing this. DON'T DO IT! I am sure I don't have to tell you why but I am going to anyway. You can chemically burn the tip of your tongue, and I am pretty sure it is the most Unhygienic thing known to man. I don't want your saliva on my soap, thank you.

The third method is to use phenolphthalein. Phenolphthalein works in solution just like all PH tests. In solution, this chemical starts to show light pink around a PH of 8.2 and darkens in the pink shade as you move up the scale. The problem is, if you are testing molten hot process soap or cold process soap shavings, they are not in an aqueous solution. The good thing about Phenolphthalein, it still works if the soap is not in solution, but the conditions are changed. Soap not in solution will test clear up to a higher level on the PH scale. Testings with my actual PH meter have indicated that soap tested out of solution with Phenolphthalein will test clear between 9 and 10.5 on the PH scale rather than starting to pinken at 8.2. What does this mean? It means you can still test for an excessively high PH level by moving the PH scale forward by 1 to 2 colour ranges. I will accept a Phenolphthalein reading out of solution of no colour to very light pink. When testing this colour scale with my PH meter, I always have landed in the range of 8 to 10 PH. Anything more vivid than a light pink, and I have a problem and discard the batch. The benefit of using this chemical out of solution is that the results are consistent rather than being all over the board as we are with PH strips. I have found this process to work well.

The fourth and fail-safe testing method is to buy an actual PH meter that comes with solution kits. You will have to decide what works best for you. There are many articles on PH testing online. If you head online for some more info, just be cautious and consider this conversation as you decide on how you will test your soap.

COLORANTS - SCENTS - ADDITIVES
Finishing Touches

"Make it. Then make it shine!"
— Brian Cockell

Once you have created your perfect base recipe or recipes, it is time to get creative with colour, scent, and even additives. These finishing touches are one of the areas where you make your soap shine and stand out from all the others out there on the market. One of the main decisions you have made at this point in your journey is what type of soapmaker you will be. Are you going to be making what is accepted as an all-natural soap, or are you going to be using some synthetics or raw materials that have a tough time fitting into the all-natural category? Considering this book is focused on all-natural soap, I will only briefly touch on non-natural scents, colours, and ingredients to help you know what to avoid or what is considered acceptable if you are going all-natural.

Colour

When making a lovely lavender soap, the finishing touch is to turn it a beautiful purple. Making a lemon soap, you will want it to be a nice yellow colour and so on. There are three main ways to colour your soap, but only one of the three is considered natural. The three primary colourants are micas, oxides, and botanicals. Never use food colouring to colour your soap. Food colouring is 100 percent synthetic. It is made in a lab. It also will tend to dye washcloths, your tub or sink and skin. Also, know that you can purchase colourants from soap-making supply companies explicitly made for soap. Be aware that you should avoid these if you plan to make an all-natural soap as they are full of synthetics.

Micas

Mica is a silicate mineral found in granite, crystals, and other rocks. It is naturally occurring when found in its natural form. They generally come in powdered form. The first problem with micas is they also come in a synthetic form that is artificial. Distinguishing between the two is difficult.

The second problem is natural micas can have traces of mercury, lead and arsenic. Substances you, of course, want to avoid. The third and most significant problem with micas is, once extracted, they are mixed with the very same synthetic lab dyes, ultramarines, or iron oxides you are trying to avoid to get those vibrant colours you see.

Although many natural soapers use micas and label their soap as natural, I don't recommend it. It is misleading, and one day in the not too distant future, the governments will regulate what is acceptable as natural. I am confident that micas will not make the list of what is natural. If you are using micas when this ultimately happens, you will be forced to remove the word natural from your label or discontinue using micas and redesign your soap. Neither of these circumstances would be ideal. As customers become more educated and engaged in reading and understanding your ingredients list, you risk losing the more educated ones if micas appear on your label. For these reasons, I do not recommend micas to colour your soap.

Iron Oxide

Many natural soapers use iron oxides; however, they suffer the same fate as micas. Although natural oxides are extracted from the earth, the final product has been heavily processed in a lab and is a hybrid of natural and synthetic. There are also synthetic "nature identical" oxides produced solely in a lab, and once again, distinguishing between the two is difficult. Unprocessed oxides also have a very high mineral content. To be used in cosmetics, the FDA requires them to be processed as above. Iron oxides generally come in powdered form. I think iron oxides will not make the list of what is natural once the government gets around to regulating the term, putting you at risk as above to either have to remove natural from your label or remove the oxides and redesign your soaps.

Botanicals

The fail-safe colour for both safety and mitigating your risk of changing labels or ingredients in the future due to regulations is botanicals. Botanicals also have great label appeal for your customers, and there is no debate over their authenticity of being natural. When you use a botanical, you also impart the beneficial characteristics of your chosen botanical into your soap.

So what is a botanical colour, and how do you achieve it? A botanical colour is just as indicated—a ground plant, nut, or herb. You can use ground seeds, ground roots, ground leaves, ground spices, etc. There are two main ways to use botanicals as a colourant. The first is to use a finely ground seed, root or herb.

A good example is to add finely ground alkanet powder to your soap right after you have reached trace to get a nice purple colour in your soap. As you mix your alkanet powder into your batter, it will turn a lovely light purple. How much you use will dictate how deep of a purple colour you achieve. Another example would be to use ground annatto seed. A little annatto seed mixed into your soap batter will give you a lovely yellow soap. A lot of ground annatto seed will provide you with a vibrant orange soap. A top-rated soap today is activated charcoal soap. You would mix activated charcoal powder into your soap for a nice black or grey colour for this soap. Many ground botanicals are available on the market that you can use in your soap to achieve great colours.

The only thing you need to be aware of is some botanicals will turn brown and not achieve the colour you are looking for when exposed to lye. The one way around this problem is to add the ground seed mixed into a little oil or water after a hot process soap has been cooked and fully saponified (no lye left in it) and before you mould it. Some ground botanical seeds cannot be used with cold process soap.

I have included a chart on the next page with some good options for ground seeds and what colour they will give you. This chart shows the ground seed, where to mix the ground seed – in the pot after the cook, in your heated oils or the lye water mixture, how much to use as a starting point based on a 10 bar cook, and what type of soap it can be used in, hot process, cold process or both.

Soap Colorant Powders			
Colorant	**Final Colour**	**Usage**	**Per Kg soap**
Alkanet Root Powder	Purple	Mix Root in carrier oil	1 Teaspoon
Annatto Seed Powder	Yellow	Mix seed powder in carrier oil	1/4 Teaspoon
Annatto Seed Powder	Orange	Mix seed powder in carrier oil	3/4 Teaspoon
Cocoa Powder	Beige	Add to soap at trace	1 Teaspoon
Deep Sea Mud	Greenish Brown	Add to soap at trace	1 Tablespoon
Cosmetic Clays	Multiple	Mix with Lye/water	1 Tablespoon
Madder Root Powder	Pink	Mix with Lye/water	1/2 Teaspoon
Madder Root Powder	Red	Mix with Lye/water	1 Teaspoon
Kelp or Sage Powder	Light Green	Mix into soap after cooking - Not for CP	2 teaspoons
Spirulina Powder	Turquoise green	Mix into soap after cooking - Not for CP	1.5 Teaspoons

You can also use botanicals to infuse your oils. Infusing plant leaves in oil is a popular method to get a nice colour, although usually not as vibrant as using ground seeds. An example of infusion would be to add nettle leaves or sage leaves to one of your oils. You would then gently simmer your infused oil for a couple of hours on your stove or induction burner. You can also set the infused oil in the window in direct sunlight for a day or so. I prefer the simmering method, as exposing your oils to direct sunlight can shorten their shelf life. You can also store an infused oil out of direct sunlight, but the infusion process will take upwards of one or two weeks to achieve your desired colour. In the above methods, the longer the infusion time, the more vibrant the colour.

After the infusion time, you would strain the plant matter out of the oil, and it is ready to be used in your soap. A coffee strainer works well. As an example, nettle leaves or sage leaves will give you a lovely light green soap. Great for a spearmint or wintergreen soap. The stronger the infusion, the stronger the colour.

Scents

Scenting your soap is one of the finishing touches that will make your product unique to your business and help you stand out above the crowd. There is nothing more pleasing to see a customer pick up your soap, give it a sniff, and then smile ear to ear with a look of pleasure on their face. Great scents sell soap!

There are two main ways to scent your soap. You can either use fragrance oils or essential oils. Fragrance oils are made in a lab and are predominantly synthetic compounds. They are created to mimic natural scents with nothing natural about them. Again, if you intend to make an all-natural soap, you will want to avoid synthetic fragrances.

Essential oils are all-natural. They are the lifeblood of plants and also impart therapeutic benefits to your soap. Essential oils are classified by what is called their note. The classifications are high, middle and base notes. Most high notes lose their scent quickly, with some exceptions. Middle notes and base notes maintain their scent longer. If using a high note essential oil, you will want to mix it with a mid or base note to prolong the scent life in your soap. Some exceptions to this rule would be essential oils like cinnamon, spearmint, peppermint, eucalyptus and lemongrass. Although beyond the scope of this book, there are many great resources out there to learn about essential oils and their therapeutic values and usage. I have included a chart below to show you which essential oils fit into which note category.

Essential Oil Notes		
High	**Middle**	**Base**
Basil (To Middle)	Bay	Balsam Peru
Bergamot	Black Pepper	Cassia
Cajuput	Cardamom	Cedarwood
Cinnamon	Chamomile	Cinnamon
Clary Sage	Cypress	Clove
Coriander	Fennel	Frankincense
Eucalyptus	Geranium	Ginger
Grapefruit	Ho Leaf	Jasmine
Hyssop	Ho Wood	Myrrh
Lemon	Hyssop	Oakmoss
Lemongrass	Juniper	Patchouli
Lime	Lavender	Rose
Mandarin	Marjoram	Rosewood
Neroli	Melissa	Sandalwood
Niaouli	Myrtle	Valerian
Orange	Nutmeg	Vanilla
Peppermint	Palma Rosa	Vetiver
Petitgrain	Pine	Ylang Ylang
Ravensara	Rosemary	
Sage	Spikenard	
Spearmint	Yarrow	
Tagetes		
Tangerine		
Tea Tree		
Thyme		
Verbena		

When adding essential oils to hot or cold process soap, you add the oils just before the soap is put into the mould. The lye in hot process soap has been neutralized at this point, and your oils are not damaged in any way. There will be some scent loss in cold process soap due to it being exposed to lye. If you put equal amounts of essential oil in both hot and cold process soap, your hot process soap will have a stronger scent. If you want to maintain the same scent in a cold process soap, you will need to add more of your essential oil. You will lose some of your essential oils to the high heat during the curing process when curing cold process soap.

You scent your soap to achieve your preferred scent. The more essential oil you put in your soap, the stronger the scent. Most soapers use a combination of essential oils to achieve that perfect scent. You will want to take a look at any regulations around quantities of essential oils used. Some countries will have a maximum usage amount. I generally scent my soap using around 2% for my essential oils quantity. You will use trial and error to develop your soap recipes to achieve what you consider that perfect scent.

There can be too much of a good thing. Putting too much essential oil in a soap batch can have a negative effect on some customers with sensitive skin, so do not go too crazy with your essential oils.

Additives

Additives are one area where you can speak to ten different soapers and get ten different answers. Some use them, and some don't. What are additives?
There are two main types. Functional and esthetic. Certain additives are great for label appeal and pique customers' interest in your soap.

A functional additive is an ingredient you put into your soap to improve on a base recipe, impart a characteristic to your soap like more bubbles, or change the function of the soap to be, say, exfoliating. You can experiment with different additives or a combination of them and be very creative. You can also use additives to achieve a specific result you are seeking to accomplish with your soap. For example, if you want your soap to last longer and your bars a little harder, you can add stearic acid to achieve this goal without changing the oils in your base recipe. If you want more slip and glide in your soap, you can add some kaolin clay and so on.

An esthetic additive is an item you add to your soap to make it look cool. For example, you could sprinkle oatmeal on the top of your bars just after moulding to give it a unique novelty look. Another popular method of using esthetic additives is to cut or shape a different colour soap into little blocks or circles or shapes and embed these shapes into your batter at moulding to have coloured embeds in your soap. An esthetic additive changes the appearance of your soap but does not alter your soap characteristics.

You will mainly find novelty soap makers adding esthetic additives to their soaps. In my experience, customers appear to consider soap with a bunch of esthetic additives in it as a gifting or decorative soap for a spare bathroom and not a soap they would use every day. Keep this in mind when designing your business plan and the types of soap you will make. There is nothing wrong with having a novelty line of soap, but I would not make this your main focus or product line as you will find yourself very limited in overall sales.

On the next page, you will find two charts for additives, how to use them, and what characteristics they impart to your soap. These are not definitive lists. Soapers are always coming up with great ideas and new additives to improve their soaps. These lists are a starting point for you to experiment with as you design your perfect bar of soap. When working with new additives, always pre-determine how they react with lye before using them. You don't want your soap to turn brown or have a nasty odor which is possible if an additive is not lye friendly. As discussed above, putting additives into cooked hot process soap is not a problem as the lye is saponified. I have included a list of additives for liquids and another for general additives on the next page.

Liquid Additives - Replacing Water			
Additive	Adds	Usage	Additive/Water %
Milk	Moisturization/Creamy/Bubbles	Mix frozen into water - Add Lye	80/20
Goats Milk	Mositurization/Creamy/Bubbles	Mix frozen into water - Add Lye	80/20
Juice	Bubbles	Mix with water - Add Lye	20/80
Beer	Bubbles/Conditioning	Simmer out Alcohol - Add Lye	100/0
Wine	Bubbles	Simmer out Alcohol - Add Lye	100/0

General Additives			
Additive	**Adds**	**Usage**	**Add Per 1 Kg of Soap Batter**
Clay - All Types	Slip and glide	Blend with water - Add Lye	30g
Silk Powder	Slip and glide	Blend into essential oils	16g
Sugar	Lather	Blend with water - Add Lye	10g
Salt	Hardness	Blend with hot Lye solution	10g
Stearic Acid	Hardness	Blend into heated oils	15g
Activated Charcoal	Detoxing	Blend into Lye solution	1g
Coffee Grounds	Exfoliant	Grind fine - Add to oils	15g
Nuts - Seeds	Exfoliant	Grind fine - Add to oils	15g
Oats - Grains	Exfoliant	Grind fine - Add to oils	15g
Pumice	Exfoliant	Grind fine - Add to oils	10g
Corn Meal	Exfoliant	Grind Fine - Add to cooked Batter	15g
Egg Shells	Exfoliant	Grind Fine - Add to cooked Batter	15g

PRICING & PROFIT
Making Money

"Big is not always good, as in – I had a
big loss.
I had a big profit sounds much better."
— Brian Cockell

YOU HAVE PUT YOUR BUSINESS STRUCTURE IN PLACE. You have set up your soap studio, and the required production equipment is in place. You have collected your raw materials, and you are either ready to start making soap or have already started and have already built up some inventory. The next big question is, what will be the price of your soap? What will your profit margins be? How much money are you going to make?

Pricing your soap is the single most crucial decision you will make. I have seen many new artisan soap companies come and quickly go for two reasons. Firstly, they do not understand the actual cost of producing a bar of soap. Secondly, they sell their soap too cheap.

Before you can set a price for your soap, you need to know how much money each bar will cost you. To understand this, you have to know the cost of each of the following per bar of soap:

Raw materials
label
Packaging
Labour
Overheads

There are several ways to calculate and track your costs. You can use the simple method of using a spreadsheet created by hand or an electronic spreadsheet program like Excel or an equivalent. You can use an industry-specific program like SoapMaker3. You can use the more complex method of using an accounting program. I will touch on all three.

Using a spreadsheet like Excel or its equivalent is very easy if you know how to work around these programs. If you do not have any experience with spreadsheets, now is the time to learn how to use them if this is the route you have decided to go for your costing. There are many free tutorials online, and most spreadsheet programs also have tutorials built right into them. I have created a quick hands-on tutorial if you would like to learn how to use Excel. Most spreadsheet programs are very similar. If you can use one, you can most likely use them all. You can find a link to this free tutorial in the Appendix.

If you do not own Excel or an equivalent, a great free office suite is called "OpenOffice." This office suite is a free download at https://www.openoffice.org and includes a word processor like Office, a spreadsheet program like Excell, and a Powerpoint program like PowerPoint. Simply download the program and open up the spreadsheet program. Its functionality is almost identical to Excel, so you will be able to follow along with the below instructions or my video tutorial on YouTube. There are many other free spreadsheet programs available. If you do an online search for "Free spreadsheets," an extensive list will come up.

Using Excel or an equivalent

If you know how to make a spreadsheet, you can skip to the end of this section to the final result and the completed costing sheet for the lavender soap we made in our recipe above.

If you want to learn about spreadsheets, you can continue reading this section or head over to my YouTube spreadsheet tutorial found in the Appendix. My YouTube video is easier to follow along with and a little more detailed. Otherwise, keep reading and following along. If you do head over to YouTube, when you come back to the book, pick the chapter up at the picture of the completed lavender soap costing spreadsheet a little further down.

Spreadsheet programs consist of columns and rows. The intersection of a column and row is called a cell. You enter your information and data into the cells. Some data is informational, like titles. Other pieces of information are data or formulas to manipulate data by adding, subtracting, multiplying, or dividing it for an answer. Although this sounds complicated, it is not. We will walk through the creation of a simple spreadsheet to price our soap.

Columns are indicated by the the alpha characters at the top of the spreadsheet working area. Rows are indicated by the numbers on the left-hand side of the spreadsheet. The below graphic of an Excel spreadsheet has 18 rows, and the columns go from A to J. A Cell is indicated by the green box at the intersection of column A and row 1, referred to as Cell A:1. All Cells have a column and row intersection. The little red star you see in the graphic below is in Cell G:10. You reference each cell by these intersecting numbers and alpha characters.

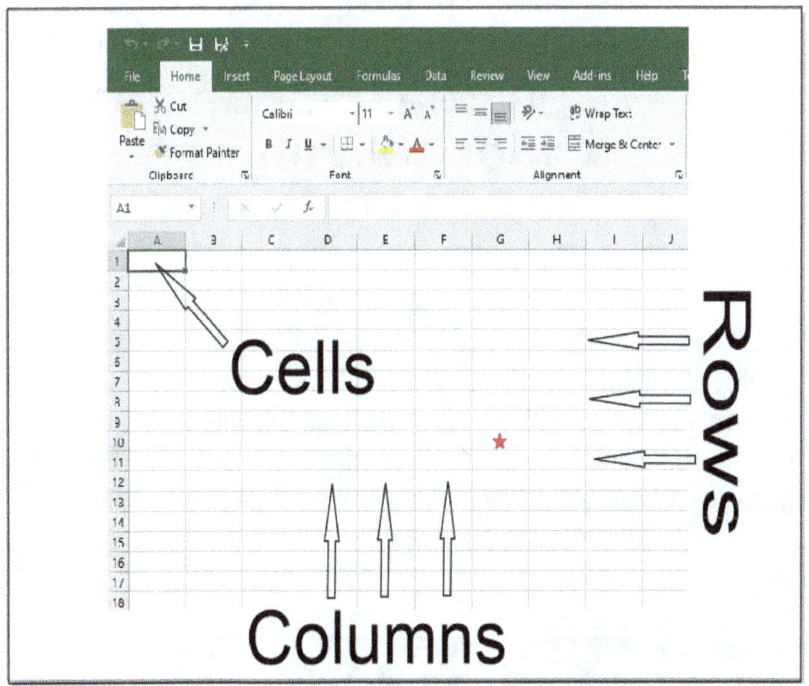

Image 1

You make rows and columns bigger or smaller by placing your cursor on the line between the letters or numbers, holding left click on the mouse, and then dragging the line left or right for columns or up and down for rows. You will want to make rows or columns bigger or smaller to fit the title or data you are putting into the cells.

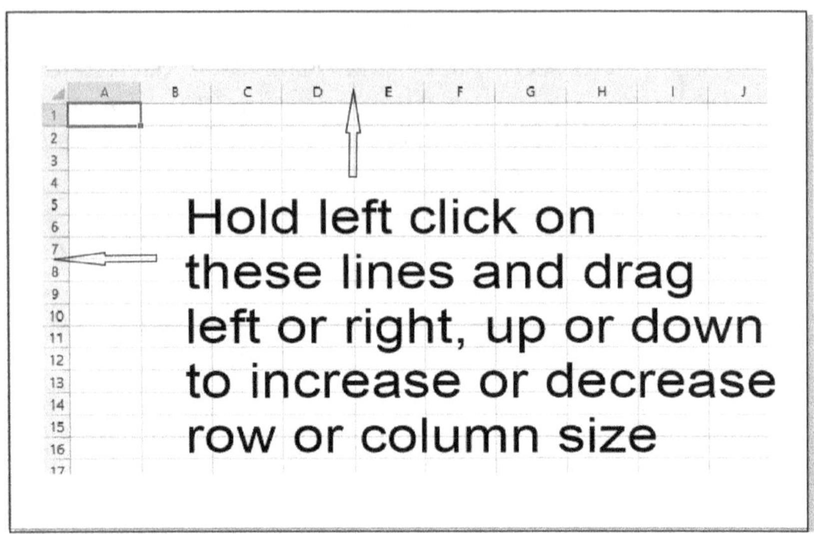

Image 2

Ok, let's make a costing sheet for our soap. Open up your spreadsheet program and open a new blank workbook. Do this by left-clicking on "File" in the menu bar and then left-click on "New" and then left-click on "Blank Workbook." There are many ways to accomplish the same thing. I will only describe one method for each task as we go through this tutorial.

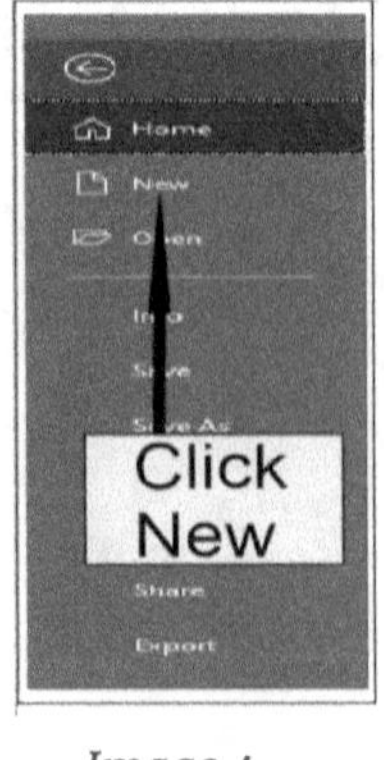

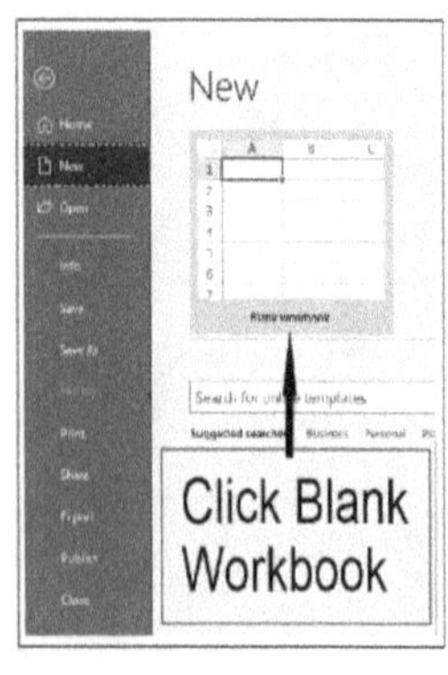

Image 3

Image 4

Image 5

You can change the font size, justification and bold the text from the Home Tab as indicated in the below graphic.

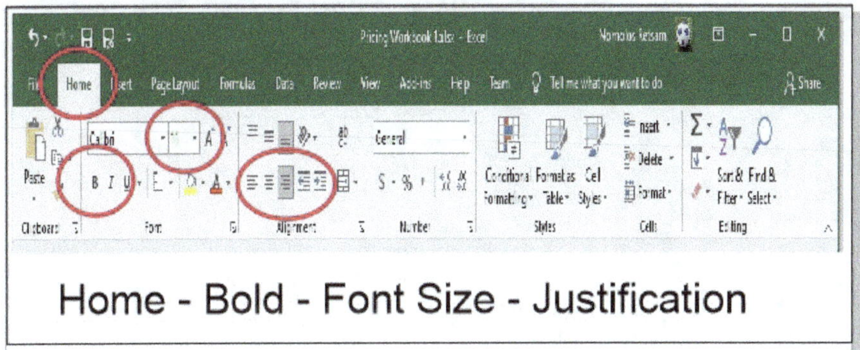

Image 6

With your spreadsheet open, enter the titles in the cells as indicated below. Expand the cells to fit the titles in row 3. Do not expand the cells in row 2. We will stretch this title across the sheet when we are putting on the finishing touches.

	A	B	C	D	E	F	G
1							
2		Soap Costing Sheet					
3		Item	Units	Cost Per Unit	Total Cost		
4							
5							
6							

Image 7

Next, fill in the items in Columns B and D:25 as indicated in the graphic below.

These are the ingredients from our recipe we made in the chapter on soapmaking with the addition of "Packaging" and an "Other" category consisting of Labour and Electricity. Each of these line items is a cost to make a bar of soap.

	A	B	C	D	E	F
1						
2		**Lavender Soap Costing Sheet - 1 Bar (125g)**				
3		**Item**	**Units**	**Cost Per Unit**	**Total Cost**	
4						
5		**Raw Materials**				
6		Palm Oil				
7		Olive Oil				
8		Coconut Oil				
9		Castor Oil				
10		Stearic Acid				
11		Water				
12		Lye				
13		Kaolin Clay				
14		Lavender Essential Oil				
15		Alkanet Powder				
16						
17		**Packaging**				
18		Label				
19		Bakers Tissue				
20						
21		**Other**				
22		Labour				
23		Electicity				
24						
25				**Total Cost**		
26						

Image 8

The next thing we have to do is enter our actual weights in grams per bar of our raw materials. In our sample batch, we are making 4 bars of soap. In our costing sheet, we are costing out 1 bar of soap, so each quantity will need to be divided by 4.

All formulas begin with an equal sign. We will take the total number of grams in our recipe for palm oil and divide it by 4 to give us how many grams go into 1 bar of soap. To type a formula into a cell, click on the cell that you want to work with. You will see a border around your active cell. The formula will look like this and be typed exactly as you see it into cell C:6.

=171/4 This formula represents 171 grams of olive oil divided by 4.

That's it. Your total weight divided by 4 gives you the weight of one bar for palm oil. You should see the number 42.75 in cell C:6 after entering the formula above into Cell C:6. Each of the ingredients will follow the same formula rule. I will give you one more, and then you can go ahead and create the formulas for each raw material in your spreadsheet. Don't forget the = sign and the / symbol represents division.

For olive oil, from our recipe, 4 bars are 144 grams of oil, so in Cell C:7, divide 144 by 4. Your formula to enter into cell C:7 will look like this.

=144/4

Once you have entered this formula and hit enter, you should now have a value of 36 in cell C:7.

Go ahead and enter all the formulas, each ingredient divided by 4 in the corresponding C cell beside its name. The only exception is the alkanet powder. Because we use so little of it, we are unable to weigh it properly, so in this case, just enter 1 gram in cell C:15

For the packaging section, you will use 1 label and 1 baker's tissue for our example. Each bar of soap will be wrapped in 1 tissue paper and wrapped with 1 label. Enter a 1 in Cells C:18 and C:19. You do not need to use an equal sign before the number when you are merely entering a number. You only use an equal sign to create a formula to calculate the result of a math equation on 2 or more numbers.

For Labour and Electricity, also enter a 1 in each of the corresponding C Cells. We will discuss how to calculate the actual cost in the next column. For now, we will assume 1 unit of each. Enter a 1 in Cells C:22 and C:23.

Once you have made all these entries, your spreadsheet should look like the graphic below. You will notice on your spreadsheet that some of your numbers are more than two decimal places. Since we are working to 1/10 of a gram, we only need 1 decimal place for our raw materials, and we will want 2 decimal places for our dollar figures. To change your Cells in column C to 1 decimal place, do the following:

Place your mouse cursor in cell C:6 and hold down left click. Holding left click, drag your mouse down column C until you reach Cell C:23. Now release the left mouse button. These Cells will now be highlighted—Right-click within this highlighted area to bring up a menu box. When you see the menu box, left-click on "Format Cells," This will bring up a selection box. Under the tab "Number," you will see a selection choice called "Number." Click on this selection, and then you will see a "Decimal Places" box with a 2 in it. Change this 2 to a 1 and left-click on OK. Voila, now all the cells you selected only have 1 decimal point. You do not need to take this step, but it makes your spreadsheet look more professional, and you do not have to do any rounding yourself.

	Item	Units	Cost Per Unit	Total Cost
Lavender Soap Costing Sheet - 1 Bar (125g)				
Raw Materials				
	Palm Oil	42.8		
	Olive Oil	36.0		
	Coconut Oil	22.5		
	Castor Oil	9.0		
	Stearic Acid	2.3		
	Water	39.4		
	Lye	15.8		
	Kaolin Clay	1.0		
	Lavender Essential Oil	3.4		
	Alkanet Powder	1.0		
Packaging				
	Label	1.0		
	Bakers Tissue	1.0		
Other				
	Labour	1.0		
	Electicity	1.0		
			Total Cost	

Image 9

The next thing we have to do is calculate the unit cost for each of these items. These costs will be entered in the D column in the row of each item. As you will always create your recipes using weight rather than volume. I am working in grams. We will calculate the cost per gram for our consumables and price per unit for the "Packaging" and "Other" items. You could just as easily be working in ounces. If you do want to work in ounces, they are provided on our recipe sheet.

We will create a formula to calculate the cost per gram within the cells of the spreadsheet. All formulas begin with an = sign as stated. If you forget the equal sign, you will see what you typed in the cell, and no actual calculation will be made. Up to this point, we have looked at how to divide. Adding, Subtracting, and multiplying work the same way. These symbols are +. -. * respectively.

These formulas will look like this:

To add, =1+1
To subtract, =1-1
To multiply, =1*1

Sometimes, just like doing standard math equations, you will need to add parenthesis to force the order of operations like this:

=(1+2)*3. This formula will equal 9, forcing the addition between the parenthesis to be calculated first before the multiplication. If you did not add the parenthesis, you would have received a different result like this:

=1+2*3. Because there is no parenthesis forcing the order of operations in this formula, the multiplication will happen first with a result of 6. Then it will add 1 to the 6 giving you a result of 7. Multiplication and division are always solved before addition and subtraction unless you add parenthesis to force the order of operation.

I know we are making soap, not learning math equations, but it is essential to make a costing sheet to figure out how much each bar of soap costs so you can sell it for the right amount to make a profit. If you are having trouble here, head over to my YouTube video on making a costing sheet. It is a little easier to follow.

Ok, back to our regularly scheduled program

We now need to calculate the cost per gram for each of our raw materials and enter this cost per gram in column D beside the row of your raw material. You will need to know two pieces of information. How many grams or ounces are in the containers of raw materials you are using, and what you paid for it.

For example, I use 5-kilogram tubs of palm oil and pay $26,00 per tub. I know there are 1000 grams per kilogram, so the number of grams in my tub of palm oil is 5000 grams. If I divide my cost of $26.00 by 5000, I will have my price per gram. We can do this in a formula like this:

=26/5000. The result will be 0.0052.

This is my cost per gram for palm oil.

I will give you a cheat sheet below for the formulas you will need to enter into our costing sheet based on my raw material costs. Go ahead and enter these formulas now in column D beside each raw material. If you have purchased your own raw materials by this point in time, go ahead and substitute your container size and cost in the formulas. Otherwise, follow along with my numbers. Your filled-in sheet should look like the below graphic if you are using my costs and container sizes.

	A	B	C	D	E
3		Item	Units	Cost Per Unit	Total Cost
5		**Raw Materials**			
6		Palm Oil	42.8	$0.0052	=26/5000
7		Olive Oil	36.0	$0.0044	=22/5000
8		Coconut Oil	22.5	$0.0093	=28/3000
9		Castor Oil	9.0	$0.0066	=26.2/4000
10		Stearic Acid	2.3	$0.0097	=9.69/1000
11		Water	39.4	$0.0005	=2.25/5000
12		Lye	15.8	$0.0031	=78/25000
13		Kaolin Clay	1.0	$0.0065	=6.5/1000
14		Lavender Essential Oil	3.4	$0.1280	=128/1000
15		Alkanet Powder	1.0	$0.0120	=1.2/100
17		**Packaging**			
18		Label	1.0	$0.0515	=51.5/1000
19		Bakers Tissue	1.0	$0.0075	=7.5/1000
21		**Other**			
22		Labour	1.0	$0.0938	=15/160
23		Electicity	1.0	$0.0133	=2/160
25				**Total Cost**	

Image 10

The next step to complete our costing sheet is to multiply our total grams for each of our raw materials by the cost per gram. This math will be completed in column E for each raw material giving us a total cost for a bar of soap. We will then add the multiplication for our "Packaging" and "Other" costs. The final step for column E will be to add all of our costs up in Cell E:25 to give us our total cost of 1 bar of Lavender soap.

To multiply two Cells together, we will use the simple formula of:

=Cell * Cell

For our palm oil, the formula will look like this:

=C6*D6

You will enter that formula into cell E6, giving you a total cost of $0.22 for palm oil. We will complete the same formula pattern down column E for each item.

For example, our olive oil row 7's formula typed into E:7 will look like this:

=C7*D7

Go ahead and follow this template for each row to have a total cost for each item.

In Cell E:25, type this formula exactly as below. Don't forget the = sign.

=sum(E6:E23)

This formula is how you add multiple cells together in either a column or a row.

Once you enter all the formulas for column E, your spreadsheet should now look like the graphic below. We have now completed the basic work to give us a cost per bar of soap, and the …..Drum Roll.…. cost per bar is $1.46. This cost does not include shipping. I do not include shipping in my costing sheets because I add it once an order is made based on the total weight of the order and where it is going. I then pass this cost on to the customer. The other reason not to add shipping in a costing sheet is sometimes you do not have any shipping costs. A couple of examples of this are if your customers pick orders up from your location or sell at a local artisan or farmers market. There is no shipping in these circumstances.

I have calculated labour at $15.00 per hour with an hourly production rate of 160 bars of soap. Although you will most likely be making your soap on day one and have no employees, you still need this cost built-in for when you do have employees, not to mention, you do need to get paid.

Electricity is calculated at the cost of $2.00 per hour divided by 160 bars of soap production per hour. This is assuming the use of crockpots, a stick blender, and lights.

Lavender Soap Costing Sheet - 1 Bar (125g)			
Item	**Units**	**Cost Per Unit**	**Total Cost**
Raw Materials			
Palm Oil	42.8	$0.0052	$0.22
Olive Oil	36.0	$0.0044	$0.16
Coconut Oil	22.5	$0.0093	$0.21
Castor Oil	9.0	$0.0066	$0.06
Stearic Acid	2.3	$0.0097	$0.02
Water	39.4	$0.0005	$0.02
Lye	15.8	$0.0031	$0.05
Kaolin Clay	1.0	$0.0065	$0.01
Lavender Essential Oil	3.4	$0.1280	$0.43
Alkanet Powder	1.0	$0.0120	$0.01
Packaging			
Label	1.0	$0.0515	$0.05
Bakers Tissue	1.0	$0.0075	$0.01
Other			
Labour	1.0	$0.0938	$0.09
Other	1.0	$0.1200	$0.12
		Total Cost =	**$1.46**

Image 11

Once I finish a draft of a spreadsheet like the one we are working on, I will then go in and put some final touches on it before calling it complete. Although the sheet above is fine and gives us the information we are looking for, I like a more professional look and feel to my work. I will not cover how to do this here, but if you would like some further instruction on how to make your sheets look professional, head on over to my YouTube tutorial, which covers the final touches. A finalized sheet looks like the graphic below and is ready for saving or printing.

Here is a graphic of my final costing sheet cleaned up and looking very professional.

Lavender Soap Costing Sheet - 1 Bar (125g)			
Item	**Units**	**Cost Per Unit**	**Total Cost**
Raw Materials			
Palm Oil	42.8	$0.0052	$0.22
Olive Oil	36.0	$0.0044	$0.16
Coconut Oil	22.5	$0.0093	$0.21
Castor Oil	9.0	$0.0066	$0.06
Stearic Acid	2.3	$0.0097	$0.02
Water	39.4	$0.0005	$0.02
Lye	15.8	$0.0031	$0.05
Kaolin Clay	1.0	$0.0065	$0.01
Lavender Essential Oil	3.4	$0.1280	$0.43
Alkanet Powder	1.0	$0.0120	$0.01
Packaging			
Label	1.0	$0.0515	$0.05
Bakers Tissue	1.0	$0.0075	$0.01
Other			
Labour	1.0	$0.0938	$0.09
Other	1.0	$0.1200	$0.12
		Total Cost =	**$1.46**

Image 12

We now know what it will cost to produce one bar of lavender soap (using my costs). As you sell more soap, your raw materials costs will reduce because you will make volume purchases at lower prices. You will also find better deals with larger companies as your business grows. You will want to save your costing sheets in a costing file to make adjustments as your costs adjust.

So what should you sell your soap for? This is the million-dollar question, literally. Today, the "All-Natural" customer understands that natural products cost a little more than store-bought synthetics. They also understand that "Hand-Made" natural products also come with an additional premium—good news for you and your new venture.

Most new soap makers do not make it because they underprice their products. Don't make this mistake, or your new business will be short-lived. Do not be scared to sell your natural hand-made soap at a good profit. If you make a great soap with a lovely scent and a great-looking package, your customers will buy it and keep coming back for more.

I can't tell you what to sell your soap for as I do not know your actual costs or what markets you plan to tackle. I will tell you how much I sell my soap for and all our other products. I first take my cost and then multiply it by 4. I then round up to the nearest dollar figure. That's it, a simple formula that I apply to all my products and produces a very reasonable return. My simple formula looks like this:

$1.35 X 4 = $5.40 rounded up to the closest dollar = $6.00

I sell all my all-natural soap for $6.00, my Goat's milk soap for $7.00, and my all-natural organic soap for $8.00. People buy it online and at artisan markets all day long at these prices and return for more. If nothing else, sell your soap for what it is worth. Set your pricing to make a good profit. This advice is the biggest takeaway from the book!

SALES & MARKETING
Selling Your Soap

"Don't celebrate closing a sale. Celebrate opening a relationship."
— Patricia Fripp

SELLING YOUR SOAP, where the rubber meets the road. The biggest asset to your business is you! No one will be better equipped or have the same motivation that you have to sell your soap. You are the front person for your business. When it comes to a sales and marketing plan, let your creative juices flow.

Marketing Tools

Presenting your business and yourself to your customers comes in many forms. Your first consideration is your marketing tools. Marketing tools are a logo for your business, possibly a brand logo, business cards, letterhead, posters, flyers, and banners, to name a couple. You can either have a professional graphics art studio help you with these items or do the bulk of your work yourself.

To have a studio help you with this, find an excellent local company and develop a relationship with them. They will sit down with you to have you share your vision with them on the above items. They will then create a couple of options to review and then adjust with your input. Once you have decided on a logo and your advertising items, they will either print on your instructions or send the work out to a printer. As you can imagine, this is a costly option and outside of the financial capabilities of most who are starting a business.

The better option is to create these items on your own and then send your artwork to a local or national printer to have them printed. Many online companies do printing at a very reasonable price. One such company would be Vista Print. This is a very inexpensive option but, of course, will take some work on your part. Doing your own work is easier than you might think. We talked about a graphics art program in the labelling chapter to make your own labels. My chosen program is the Corel Suite of Programs for all the reasons listed in the labelling chapter.

Within this program, you can create everything you need as far as artwork is concerned and even print some items in-house like letterhead. Invoices and envelopes. Doing a graphics art tutorial within the pages of this book would not work; however, if you want to create your own artwork for your advertising materials, I have created a YouTube video to teach you how and walk you through the process. You can find a link to this video in the Appendix. Below are a couple of the items I use that I created in Corel Draw and had printed at Vista Print. Each of these items and how to create them, meaning your version, is covered in my graphic arts YouTube tutorial.

Our Company Logo

Image 1

Our Business Cards

Image 2 *Image 3*

Advertising Banners Used at Artisan & Farmers Markets

Image 4 –5 –6

Swag

Image 7   Image 8   Image 9

Creating your own Logo, stationary, and advertising materials are fun and rewarding. Your only limitation is your imagination. Whichever route you go, doing it yourself or having someone do it for you, it is essential to create both professional and inviting advertising and stationery. It is how people will come to recognize you and your company. When we attend artisan or farmers' markets, we can see prior customers on the other side of the show or market pointing at our signage and heading our way.

Your next big decision is to decide where your products will sell. The options are almost limitless. One of your goals will be to develop as many markets as you can. You want to have your products exposed to as many people in as many places feasible. The greater your exposure, the more products you will sell.

Friends and Family

Every new soapmaker ultimately starts giving friends and family products to test and comment on as recipes are developed and adjusted. Once you have your final product line, it is time to start selling to your close contacts. Your friends and family will understand that you are starting and running a business and will expect that they will have to pay for your products although, they will expect a discount. Don't make the mistake of giving everything away free to your close contacts. Every bar of soap you do not get paid for costs you money out of your pocket. Would you walk up to a coworker and, out of the blue, just hand them six bucks? Probably not. This is essentially what you will be doing every time you give a bar of soap away free. After your initial freebies are given out, I strongly recommend that you start to charge your close contacts for your products. We offer friends and family a standard 30% discount, and they are thrilled with that amount. They understand we are running a business.

Artisan Markets

After you have developed a thriving market with family, friends and coworkers, you will want to start to branch out to artisan markets. There will be many artisan markets in your local area. Some will be one-off shows, others will be seasonal weekly bookings, and others will run year long.

Search the internet for your local markets. Most have online applications required to be filled in several months before the event starts. It also helps to determine who the market manager is and to make direct contact with this person. You will want to introduce yourself and your products and begin to establish a relationship with them. You will want to find out if they currently have any soapmakers and, if so, how many. Do not be afraid of competition. If you have gone through this book and taken steps to prepare your business and products correctly, you will be well ahead of 90% of the soapmakers out there. We love having a couple of soapmakers at our markets. It allows our customers to make comparisons, and 9 out of 10 times, they shop with us. If there are more than four soapmakers, we will generally pass on the market. Once you reach four or more soapmakers in a market, it becomes too tedious for customers to try and compare each soapmaker. Potential customers will make purchases before reaching your booth if you are not in the most choice area. You will also want to understand the entry fee for the particular market you are looking at joining. Market entry fees can range from 10 to 300+ dollars.

You want to choose markets with high traffic. We look for markets that are going to have a minimum of 500 people per day. We have attended markets with 10,000 people coming through. The more people, the more you sell. You also want to establish a good relationship with the market manager to be awarded a spot in the market that is in a high traffic area. The last thing you want is to be stuck behind a pole in a dead-end hallway with no traffic.

You will ultimately want to accept credit and debit cards for these markets. If you cannot offer people sales with a credit or debit card, you will turn some customers away and limit your total sale per customer. There are several good choices out there. We use Square. Square comes with a card reader and point of sale software (POS) to enter your products and make credit and debit card transactions. You can also track all sales through the Square POS and receive a daily, weekly, monthly, and annual sales report. Square also allows you to take credit card payments over the phone, and it integrates well with a payment option on your website (To be discussed shortly). The fees are very reasonable for the service. I have created a YouTube video on setting up square as a payment provider and setting up and using their POS. You can find the link to this video in the Appendix.

Paypal also has a Point of Sale application that you can use to take credit cards, and there are several private companies also offering the service. You can find all your options in your area by doing an internet search for "payment providers."

Artisan markets are a great way to build a loyal customer base and eventually will be used to drive customers to your website in the off-season (Discussed in a bit). Some examples of artisan markets are:

Farmers Markets

These markets usually run once per week from mid-spring to mid-fall. A market manager runs your local farmer's market. There are generally between 20 to 30 weekly markets for the seasonal farmers market through the spring to fall. They can run on different days of the week. We usually do 5 to 6 farmer's markets per week during the selling season. You will want to have a 10x10 foot tent, folding tables and table cloths, displays for your products, and a cash register with a float for these markets. They usually run outdoors and are open, rain or shine. Once you sign up for a season, market managers will expect you to show up and set up each week. Farmer's market entry fees typically come in around the 200 to 300 dollar range for the season. This fee puts your weekly table fee between 20 to 30 dollars—a very reasonable price. You will find that you will develop a very loyal following from your local farmer's markets. For most attendees, it is an experience and social gathering as much as a sales venue.

Artisan Crafting Markets

Artisan markets are very similar to farmers' markets; however, you will find a higher concentration of crafted goods and less focus on food items. Artisan markets can be seasonal or one-offs or run all year round in an indoor location and generally are in the same price range as farmer's markets.

One-Off Markets

Your one-off markets that run once or twice per year are church bazaars, legion sales, community sales, shopping malls and such. You will also find several one-off markets run through the holiday seasons like Easter, Christmas or the major holidays. Municipalities will usually hold holiday markets in the local community centre. Other good examples of one-off markets are your local fair and home and garden shows. People attend one-off markets usually for one reason; to spend money. Most one-off markets cost between 10 and 50 dollars for a booth. The exception to this is the home and garden shows and shopping malls. These types of shows can range between 100 and 500 dollars but are well worth the entry fee. They usually run from Friday afternoon through to Sunday afternoon, and you can have thousands of people pass by your booth during the weekend.

Market Shots

Website

As you begin to sell at markets, you will have customers from all over the country, and even the world, visit your booth to buy your products. One of your main goals for selling your products is to establish loyal, repeat customers. In addition to your local customers, many market customers are visiting friends or are on vacation; A popular activity is visiting the local market. How are you going to turn these customers into repeat customers? This is where your website comes in. E-commerce is growing today in leaps and bounds, and Covid-19 has brought many new customers to the E-commerce platform; shopping online. Having a website will vastly open up the potential for your business, and your sales will explode. You will want a website up and running relatively quickly once you start selling your soap. It is effortless to create a successful website. Your two options are to hire a web developer or do it yourself. Hiring a web developer can get costly. Doing it yourself is like paint by numbers today. There are many companies offering websites and website creation tools for their sites. They are very intuitive. I will not cover the steps to creating a website in this book as there are multiple online companies and tutorials to accomplish this.

I have completed a YouTube tutorial teaching you how to get up and running with a Wix, Squarespace of Shopify website from start to finish. Wix is my chosen provider for its ease of use and low cost. Below is a copy of my homepage on our LifeGeivity Soap Company website. This tutorial is for beginners and is very user-friendly. I walk you through each step of getting your site up and running, including managing shipping and payment providers like PayPal and Square. If you would like to learn more about Wix, Squarespace or Shopify and how to set up a website, head over to the YouTube tutorial found in the resource link in the Appendix.

www.lifegevitysoaps.ca

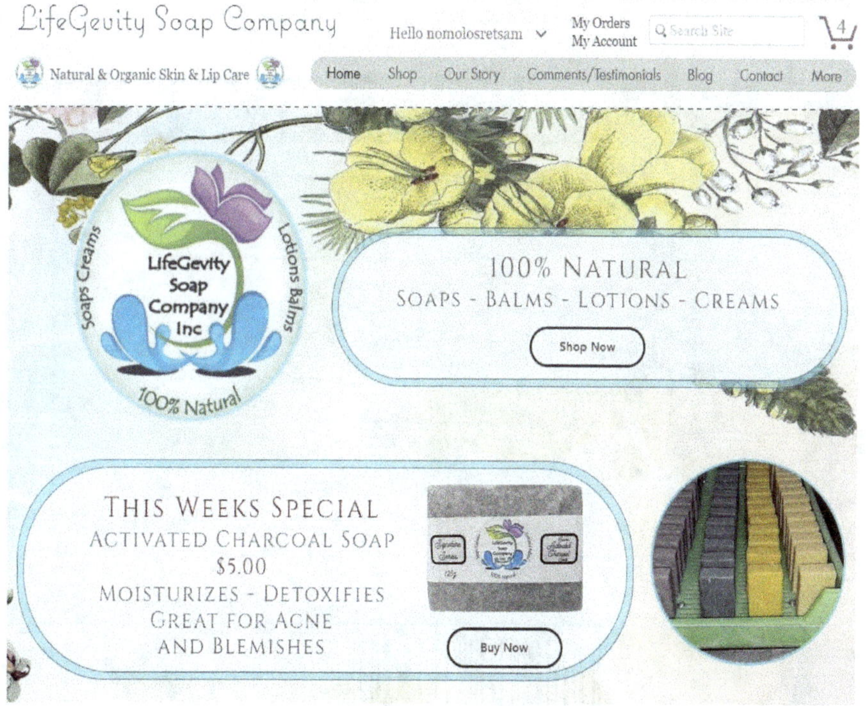

Online Retailers

You are now selling to family, friends and coworkers. You are selling at markets and have a website up and running. Your next step in your marketing plan is to get your products listed with national online sellers like Amazon and Etsy, to name a couple.

Selling on these platforms is relatively easy. You set up an account, list your products and wait for the sales to roll in. Each platform is very intuitive. Go to their websites to get started. They will walk you through the setup instructions. You will be up and running in no time. Amazon does require a monthly membership fee of around 30 dollars and takes a percentage of sales revenue based on total sales. They will also require your products to be either branded or have a United Product Code (UPC) for each product. An internet search for UPC product codes will get you to the UPC website to set up an account. It cost around 565.00 for an annual membership that provides you with 100 UPCs. Although we no longer sell on Etsy, we do sell some of our products on amazon.ca

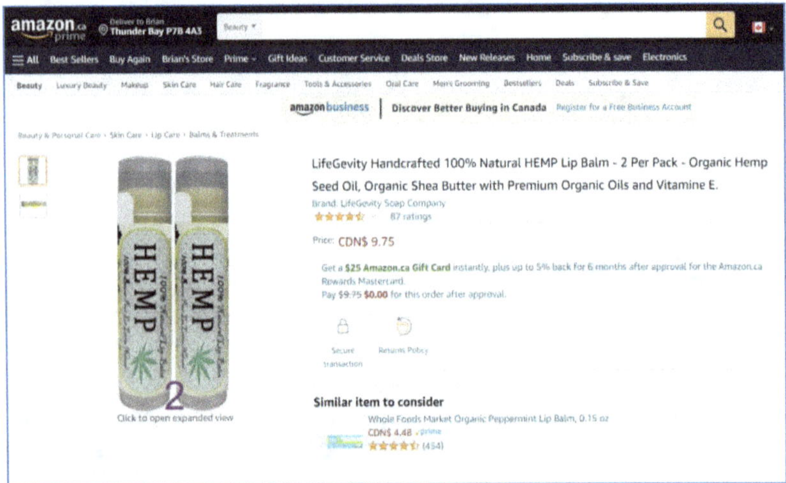

Brick and Mortar Stores

Some soapers will sell their soap to retail stores, and some won't. Retail comes with specific challenges that you do not face selling at markets, your website and online retailers. In each of these sales channels, you get paid before giving your soap to your customer or sending your product to your customers, except for Amazon. Amazon pays you every 14 days. There is no risk of losing money for non-payment.

With Brick and Mortar stores, one challenge is collecting money. Most retail outlets will require payment terms to stretch from 30 to 90+ days, meaning you send your soap to the store for sale and don't get paid right away. If the store you are selling to is having financial difficulty, you risk not getting paid at all.

Brick and Mortar stores will also require a wholesale price. Wholesale prices are set about 30% less than your retail price. Rather than selling soap at around six dollars, you will be selling soap for approximately 4.00 dollars per bar if you follow my pricing rules. This is not necessarily bad as retail store orders can be very large and worth the effort to sell at a discounted price.

There are two types of retailers. Retailers are either Ma & Pops or Chain Stores. Ma & Pops are your smaller local stores, usually family-owned, only serving the local community. You can sometimes negotiate for payment upfront with these local stores, and they are typically willing to support local businesses. They are not a bad option to sell your soap. If you plan to sell to your local Ma & Pops, go into the stores, introduce yourself, present your product line and work on establishing a relationship with the owners. Relationship selling is one of your best tools to achieving success in this area.

Chain stores are where things get interesting. Chain stores have multiple locations, either locally, regionally or nationally. Walmart or Costco are examples of big-box chain stores. Suppose you want to sell into chain stores. In that case, you will need to be well established, in business for a couple of years, and demonstrate financial viability and the ability to satisfy large orders. Chain stores will run your business through a credit check and, in most cases, require references from others you are selling. Most chain store buyers will want to tour your production facilities and verify your capacities. Chain stores have buyers who procure products for their stores. The larger chain stores have dedicated buyers for different item types.

To sell into a chain store, you will need to make an appointment with the specific buyer for your products. Getting in to see chain store buyers is a daunting task and not for the faint of heart. Ensure you are ready for a long process if you plan to get your products into these stores. Also, keep in mind that you will be competing with products from China and other offshore countries, and your price will need to be extremely low for listings with chain stores.

I do not sell into any chain stores. The risk, lower price, payment delays and effort is not worth it. Establishing a stable market and online presence is more than adequate to become an incredibly successful business in today's environment. However, if you desire to sell to the chain stores, go for it knowing the risks and effort required.

I do sell to Ma & Pops, where I can negotiate "payment on delivery" terms. Many Ma & Pops have approached us at our different markets asking to sell our products in their stores.

Creative Selling

Creative selling is where things can get fun. I define creative selling as selling your soap to unique markets. As discussed in the labelling chapter, if you are making your own labels, you are now open to offering private label packaging to customers.

Private label packaging is where you create a label specifically for a unique customer. We have been approached by local micro brewers who wanted a label with their logo on it for a beer soap, weddings that wanted soap with a picture of the bride and groom for wedding favours, wedding and baby showers, corporate conventions, on and on. Some Ma & Pop stores will get very excited about the prospect of having their store name and logo on the soap they sell. The private label market can be vast, fun and exciting, not to mention, you can charge a premium price for creating a unique label. Once again, you are only limited to your imagination.

Summary

Selling your soap is rewarding. Selling truckloads of soap is very rewarding. When you set out, create an achievable marketing plan and then work your plan. Go step by step, expanding your sales channels as you go. Learn what works well for you and what does not. Be persistent, and most importantly, think outside of the box and have fun! Before you know it, you will be selling more soap than you can make and will be contemplating expanding your business and hiring employees.

POSTSCRIPT
Nest Steps

"Your next step is your masterpiece in the making."
— Brian Cockell

You are now making and selling all-natural soap. You are on your way to running a successful business. Where do you go from here? Soapmaking is just the beginning. To build your business into that six-figure business and beyond, your next steps are to expand your product line into more all-natural skincare products. I am sure you noticed many other products in the graphics in the sales and marketing chapter. We now make and sell all-natural lip balms, hand creams, face creams, shampoo bars, deodorants, linen sprays, and we are developing a liquid soap. As our product line has grown over the years, our customer base and per-transaction sale have increased substantially.

It is estimated the natural and organic skincare market is currently sitting around 12 billion dollars in North America. The market is projected to reach 25 billion by 2025. Covid-19 is teaching people to shop online. There is an ever-growing push from customers for all-natural products as they become educated about how harmful the synthetics they are slathering on their bodies really are. It is the right business to be in at the right time, and you want a piece of it.

Most new soapers will first expand their business by adding an all-natural lip balm line. Lip balms are easy to make and package. There are no rules where you go from here—thinking about a bath bomb? Make a bath bomb. As you move into the more complicated products like creams and deodorants, you will need some guidance. This guidance is a little more challenging to come by as there is a lot of misinformation out there. Once you start creating a product with a water base, there is a whole new set of rules to get it right.

The good news is, I am currently working on my second book to help you expand your business into other products. My new book is focused on creating new products. It focuses on explaining and teaching the production process, ingredients, and recipes rather than starting a business. If you are interested in making any of the products listed above, this new book is for you as it will cover them all and then some. To get a copy of the book when it is completed, head to any of the YouTube video links in this book and join my channel. Once joined, click the little bell in the right-hand corner of the screen. You will be notified once the book is published. Your other option is to send me an email expressing interest in the new book, and I will put you on my notification list for when it is published.

The goal of this book was to share my love and deep passion for making and selling all-natural skincare products and to help you along the same journey I have travelled. I hope together we have achieved this goal. If I can help you further or have some questions, please feel free to reach out. I will do my best to respond and can be contacted at brian@lifegevitysoaps.ca

If you happened to read this book on the Amazon Kindle Prime Reading program, please consider purchasing this book outright and adding it to your library. This would help me as struggling authors only make pennies from this Amazon program.

HAPPY SOAPING! Thank you for spending this time with me. May your business flourish! I wish you all the best and great success on your journey!

Brian

Appendix

This link address will take you to the resources page for the book. Here you can find the items mentioned in the chapters, tutorial videos and additional resources.
https://www.lifegevitysoaps.ca/soap-making-resources

Excel Tutorial – Making a Costing Sheet
https://youtu.be/eHvWjhnpdJA

Recipe Tutorial
https://youtu.be/qEYTeu8Q9oQ

Soap Making Tutorial - Comprehensive
https://youtu.be/iyCvdLvafEc

Your best choices for your online eCommerce store - Instructional
https://youtu.be/svDzsITH34U

Wix eCommerce online store tutorial - Comprehensive
https://youtu.be/9AY1RUP-IT4

Wix Short eCommerce online store tutorial – Flash tutorial
https://youtu.be/ubBGQ1ZCVyw

Shopify eCommerce online store tutorial - Comprehensive
https://youtu.be/Rkx86vt5lZY

Squarespace eCommerce online store tutorial - Comprehensive
https://youtu.be/OWfT-GZTVrY